MOUNTAIN BIKE GUIDE

**Derbyshire and the
Peak District**

new edition

By
Tom Windsor
Tim Banton
Andy Spencer

D1323078

First published by The Ernest Press 1991
Reprinted 2002 with amendments
Enlarged and updated edition 1996
© Tim Banton, Tom Windsor

ISBN 0 948 153 44 X

British Library Cataloguing-in-Publication Data has been registered with
the British Library at Wetherby and is available on request.

Typeset by Val Siviter
Printed by Martins the Printers, Berwick upon Tweed

Disclaimer

Whilst we have made every effort to achieve accuracy in the production of
material for use in this guidebook, the authors, publishers and copyright
owners can take no responsibility for: trespass, irresponsible riding, any
loss or damage to persons or property suffered as a result of the route
descriptions or advice offered in this book.

The inclusion of a route in this guide does not guarantee that the path/
track will remain a right of way; if conflict with landowners occurs please be
polite and leave by the shortest possible route, then check the situation
with the relevant authority.

It is worthwhile, as a footnote to this disclaimer, to emphasise that riders
should give way to both pedestrians and horse riders and should make
every effort to warn others of their presence.

Front cover: Towards Hawks Nest (near Flash).

CONTENTS

CIRCULAR ROUTES

Acknowledgements

Thanks to: Anne and Bob Windsor, Alasdair Watson, Noel Jenkins, Shaun Masterman, Olly Stephenson, Stuart Smith, Mike Roper, Raif Killips, Brian Wyld, Patrick Watson and Bob Higginbotham for their help, whether it was test riding, encouragement, proof reading, editing, photographs or all of those things.

Thanks also to: Alan Leather, Katie Forster, Aiden Lehup, Simon Archer, Adrian Critchlow, Tony Gascoigne, Bruce and Rhona Slattery, Karin Aberg and Lottie.

The publishers acknowledge editorial and production supervision by Margot Blyth.

25 sketch maps drawn by Tim Banton. Drawings and base maps by Tom Windsor.

2002-Thanks for test riding to, Ian Banton, Aidan Leheup, Keir Windsor, John Varley, Lucy Ashworth, Tim O Neal, Ollie Penrice and Gill.

Note for the 2002 edition

The book has been around a good while now, but it's still been enjoyable to revisit the rides and check the route descriptions. On the whole all the routes could still be followed from the old descriptions. Where something important has changed like the loss of a café, or a new bit of bridleway presenting a better alternative, we have added a note at the end of the ride. Check these out before planning your ride. Minor changes such as a metal gate replacing an old wooden one, have not been addressed, but as long as you take a decent map along with you and some common sense, everything should fall into place. Hope you have as much fun on these routes as we have.

INTRODUCTION

Aims of this book
This book sets out to offer a range of circular off-road cycle rides, varying in length, difficulty and terrain, spread over Derbyshire and the Peak District. It hopes to give a taste of what the area has to offer to those who do not know it, or a different aspect for those who do. Unless stated otherwise the routes are largely rideable without dismounting. However expect to have to walk some sections now and again. Fitness, skill and ground conditions will affect the distances that you will need to walk.

Author's note to the 1996 edition
Since this guidebook was published in 1991 we have been very pleased with both how well it has sold and with the favourable comments from all sorts of people who have enjoyed the rides. For this new 1996 edition we have re-tested all the routes. We still enjoy riding them and found that they were quiet mid-week. The routes seem to have stood the test of time, most needing only minor corrections. Generally way-marking has improved and there does not seem to be a problem with excessive erosion or over-use of the trails. We have changed some of the drawings and photos and there are quite a few new cycle trails that deserve a mention.

We have added four new routes; one a very hilly gritstone ride, one a very short limestone route, a ride in the east of the county around the Bolsover area on disused railways and green lanes, and the fourth through parkland and fields on the eastern edge of Derby. We hope you will enjoy these rides too. We feel they are well worth doing and very different in feel to those already in the book.

How to use this book
The sketch maps in this book are to be used with the route description, to supplement, not replace an O.S. map. Use a large scale (1:25 000) O.S. map when riding these routes.

Grid references are used to help locate starting points. If you are unsure how to use grid references see the margin of an O.S. Outdoor Leisure map (e.g. the White Peak map) for an explanation.

The sketch maps in this book are not necessarily drawn to scale or of comparable scales with each other.

We hope the route descriptions are easy to follow. If the instructions do not say otherwise, continue on the track/path/road you are on, taking the most obvious, well-defined route.

In many of our routes we mention gates, especially if they mark a change in direction, are a landmark or are at some sort of junction. However do not assume we mention every gate. If you are following a straight track for instance, with no possibility of getting lost we may not mention the fact that you have to pass through several gates as you ride along it (though usually we will).

In our instructions we use the term five-bar gate quite loosely to describe any wide farm gate that you could drive a vehicle through. The gate may indeed have five bars but it could just as easily have two or seven.

Many of the routes could be started and finished at points other than those suggested. Sometimes they could be ridden in the opposite direction (this renders the instructions useless though the sketch map will still be useful).

Using an O.S. map you will be able to tailor routes to your own needs e.g. by making them longer, or shorter. However we think you will enjoy most of the routes as they are.

Remember
A - only ride where you have a legal right to do so.
B - you cannot tell what a bridleway or track is like on the ground by merely looking at it on a map.

Derbyshire and The Peak District

THE PEAK DISTRICT NATIONAL PARK
In 1951 the Peak District was the first National Park to be established. By merit of its position, central within Britain and surrounded by huge conurbations, it is very accessible (it is thought half the population of Britain is within sixty miles of Buxton) and consequently very heavily used (roughly twenty million visitors a year!).

Its popularity could be considered one of its main problems, one with which planners continually wrestle. However do not let this put you off. Most people travel to the Peak in, and do not stray far from, their cars. On the whole they crowd particular tourist spots. You can still find solitude on many of these off-road rides. Usually on the off-road sections you will not see more than a handful of people; sometimes no one at all.

Use public transport to, from and within the Peak Park if you can.

LANDSCAPE AND ENVIRONMENT
Derbyshire and the Peak District offer plenty for the off-road enthusiast. It is an environment of huge variety; a landscape where lowland Britain and upland Britain merge. The geology of the Peak Park can be considered in very simple terms as a downturned horseshoe-shaped section of gritstone in the north, curving down the east and west flanks, surrounding a more central area of shales and limestone.

The 'Dark Peak' area, with high moorland plateaux (peat, heather, bracken and grouse) and long dramatic gritstone edges, is juxtaposed with the very different shale and limestone features. Caves, cliffs, deep wooded dales, large quarries and lowland farms criss-crossed with mile upon mile of drystone walls are common features of the so-called 'White Peak'.

This landscape, shaped partly by climate and geology, has also been dramatically altered by man. Settlements, mill towns, factories, quarries and mines (for lead, fluorspar, coal, limestone and gritstone) as well as tourists have all made their mark and continue to do so. It's a complex but intriguing landscape as diverse and rich as many counties put together.

ACCESS AND ATTITUDE

People enjoy a wide range of outdoor pursuits in the Peak Park which are not always completely compatible. User conflict can be a problem.

With walking as one of the most popular recreations, the Peak Park Planning Board are understandably cautious in their attitude towards mountain biking. They have already had numerous problems with cyclists thinking they can ride anywhere, on footpaths and open moorland.

The 'Open Access Land' marked on O.S. maps is private land on which rights have been negotiated to walk anywhere (except in the grouse shooting season). **However cyclists have no such rights to ride on this land**, except on specific rights of way such as bridleways. Cycles have no right of way on footpaths.

Please read the section on rights of way and take heed of the two codes of conduct below. If irresponsible misuse of paths and land continues, undoubtedly mountain bikers will be restricted or banned from many areas, including those that are currently perfectly legal to ride on.

Be polite, and give way to other users. Ride responsibly. Avoid badly churned ground where possible and try not to lock your wheels especially on descents. When following the routes in this guide please keep to the defined paths and travel at a quiet and unobtrusive pace. We suggest that groups should be made up of no more than five or six cyclists. Horses are often frightened by and suspicious of bicycles, having not been in such close proximity with them before. On approaching horse riders slow to walking pace or stop and let them pass. If you want to pass ask the riders first.

THE OFF ROAD CODE

Issued by the Mountain Bike Club
- Only ride where you know you have a legal right.
- Always yield to horses and pedestrians.
- Avoid animals and crops. In some circumstances this may not be possible, at which times contact should be kept to a minimum.
- Take all litter with you.
- Leave all gates as found.
- Keep the noise down.
- Don't get annoyed with anyone; it never solves any problems.
- Always try to be self-sufficient, for you and your bike.
- Never create a fire hazard.

THE COUNTRY CODE
Issued by the Countryside Commission

- Enjoy the countryside and respect its life and work.
- Guard against risk of fire.
- Fasten all gates.
- Keep your dogs under close control.
- Keep to public paths across farmland.
- Use gates and stiles to cross fences, hedges and walls.
- Leave livestock, crops and machinery alone.
- Take your litter home.
- Help keep all water clean.
- Protect wildlife, plants and trees.
- Take special care on country roads.
- Make no unnecessary noise.

CYCLING AND CONSERVATION

The area of Derbyshire and the Peak District is a working landscape under many pressures. Farming and tourism are two major users. An increasing demand for leisure activities and wider public access to the countryside can lead to the erosion of large tracts of our landscape and the loss of valuable habitats. While out cycling you will see how various organisations are trying to tackle erosion problems. Laying huge gritstone flags from the floors of old mills (dropped in by helicopter) on wide boggy paths worn by walkers and cyclists on Howden Moor, the building of steps on Cut Gate, stone pitching and diagonal cut-off drains on Jacobs Ladder are just three examples of attempts to protect areas from over-use. Mountain bikes do cause erosion. Studies have shown that this is comparable to the damage caused by walking boots. Heavy use in wet weather is often the greatest problem; delicate habitats and ground cover being easily damaged or entirely lost.

However, I do not think we should try to preserve our landscape as some sort of pickled museum piece, to look at but not to enjoy. It is of course possible to minimise damage to the trails we use by considering where, when and perhaps most importantly how we ride. You could even be more pro-active and help by giving a practical hand...

PRACTICAL CONSERVATION PROJECTS go on throughout the area. There are many volunteer groups you can help. I have worked regularly with BTCV for the past seven years but the Peak Park, The National Trust and various Groundwork Trust all have volunteer groups too. You could help with conservation tasks that are directly linked to cycling, e.g. BTCV working holidays have this summer been working for the Peak Park using old walling stone to help drain a very boggy bridleway at Stanage Edge. Also with the Derby Midweek Conservation Volunteers I have done hedgelaying on the Melbourne Cycleway, surfacing of a new cycleway at Ironville, walling on the High Peak Trail and many other jobs. Of course many other tasks such as tree planting, pond creation, footpath work and coppicing may not be linked to cycling, but do add to the rich rural tapestry which we ride by and enjoy.

British Trust for
Conservation Volunteers

What is BTCV? - The British Trust for Conservation Volunteers is the UK's leading conservation charity enabling people to take positive action to improve the environment by doing **hands-on practical projects.**

BTCV projects can be just a day, or longer. They provide an opportunity to learn about and protect local environments and give an introduction to other conservation opportunities. There are over 100 offices around the country so there should be something going on near you. For details of your nearest local office **Tel. BTCV Head Office 01491 839766**

Many BTCV offices run residential conservation projects. **'Natural Break' working holidays;** there are more than 500, country-wide **Tel. 01491 824602.**

DERBYSHIRE BTCV run 'Countryside Weekends' and week-long holidays as well as a mid-week group. Derby Midweek Conservation Volunteers go out almost every Tuesday and Thursday throughout the year. Activities range from footpath work to stream clearance to walling or pond creation. Experience is not required, just enthusiasm and a desire to learn new skills For more details of work in Derbyshire **Tel. 01629 825317.**

PUBLIC RIGHTS OF WAY

To make the most of your off-road cycling you need to know where you can or cannot ride. In this section we hope to cover some of the basic terms you may come across to help you plan some routes of your own.

A **Public Right of Way** is a way over which all members of the public have a right to pass and repass.

PUBLIC FOOTPATH - over which there is right of way on foot only. Cyclists have **no** right of way to ride on a Public Footpath. Footpaths are sometimes waymarked on signs or marker posts by yellow arrows/discs.

BRIDLEWAY - over which there is a public right of way on foot, horseback and pedal cycle, provided that cyclists give way to horse-riders and pedestrians. Bridleways are sometimes waymarked on signs or marker posts by blue arrows/discs.

BYWAY/BOATs - open to all traffic.

RUPP - a road used as a public path. Its minimum status is usually that of a bridleway so cyclists may normally use them. However this classification has proven unsatisfactory. All RUPPs are now being reclassified as one of the above.

UNCLASSIFIED COUNTY ROAD - a minor road which may not be metalled. It can be regarded as having the same status as a byway. However they are not identified (i.e. distinguished from any other road or private track) on an O.S. map.

GREEN LANE - an unsurfaced walled track often of some antiquity. However, the term 'green lane' has no legal meaning.

TRAILS AND CYCLE TRACKS - Within Derbyshire and the Peak District are several disused railway lines which have been converted into Trails for use by the public. Many of these can be used by cyclists. See Base Map 1, and the section on trails and cycleways (pages 18 - 27).

Canal Towpaths

Many canals are owned or run by British Waterways, local councils or a combination of the two. There aren't really any hard and fast rules about which canal stretches you can or cannot ride on, and often, although they might look ideal riding on the map, they are not as straightforward on the ground. British Waterways is made up of six regions, each with a number of local offices.

To cycle on their towpaths officially requires you to send for a permit. You would also get details of which stretches of towpath you can or cannot use. Contact local offices for specific queries in order to talk to someone who actually knows the area first hand.

The Regional Office which covers most of Derbyshire and the Peak District is: N.E. Region, British Waterways, 1 Dock St., Leeds LS1 1HH. Tel. 0113 243 6741, Fax. 0113 246 5561

British Waterways Local Offices
(Erewash, Grand Union Canal, Sour Navigation, Nottingham Canal and Beeston Cut, Trent Navigation):
British Waterways, Trent Lock, Lock Lane, Long Eaton, Nottingham NG10 2FF. Tel. 0115 946 1017

(Chesterfield Canal, Sheffield and S. Yorkshire Navigation, Fossdyke and Witham Navigations, Trent Navigation, New Junction Canal, Stainforth and Keadby Canal):
British Waterways, Mill Lane, Mill Gate, Newark, Nottinghamshire NG24 4TT. Tel. 01636 704481

Although every attempt has been made in this guide for the routes to follow legal rights of way for cyclists, mistakes may have been made or changes in the network may take place. Since changes can and do occur, descriptions of routes cannot be taken as proof of a path/track being a right of way. So, if you are requested by a landowner who thinks you are trespassing, to leave the route you are following, please do not seek confrontation but be polite and leave quickly by the shortest practical route.

If you believe you were in the right, check with the correct authority and get them to deal with the problem. Above all do not give off-road cyclists a bad name.

Maps

To supplement the descriptions and maps in this guide or for planning your own off-road routes it is necessary to use good large scale maps. The Ordnance Survey publish two 1:25 000 Outdoor Leisure maps which cover most of the areas in this guide:

No. 24 - White Peak
No. 1 - Dark Peak,

which include rights of way. Other areas are covered by the Pathfinder series at the same scale.

Definitive Maps and Maps of Highways held by Local Authorities

Although public rights of way (footpaths, bridleways, RUPPs and byways) are shown on O.S. maps, changes may have taken place since they were printed. Therefore if you are in any doubt about the right of way, you should consult the Definitive Map for the area. Copies of these are held by all County Councils, Borough, District and Parish Councils. Local Libraries may well also hold copies. Unclassified roads are not recorded as being such on O.S. or definitive maps unless they are also footpaths, bridleways or RUPPs, i.e. they are not distinguishable from private tracks, drives or small roads. Since unclassified roads often provide ideal cycling it may be worthwhile consulting the county highways map which records all highways maintainable at public expense. These are held by the local highway authority and are available for public inspection at County Council offices. (See useful addresses section).

EQUIPMENT & SAFETY

A lot could be written here but too much advice is confusing to both beginner and experienced alike. So briefly:

First Aid
Knowing some basic first aid is always valuable, if not for yourself, then for those you are with or might encounter. Courses run by organisations such as the Red Cross or St. Johns Ambulance are probably the best way to learn some first aid.

A small first aid kit might include: plasters, a small roll of micropore tape, medi-wipes, a selection of bandages, some scissors and toilet paper.

Personal Identification
If you should ever have, or become involved in a serious accident, having some form of identification with you is helpful for many reasons. For example it is important to know whether a patient is: asthmatic, diabetic, allergic to penicillin or has a rare blood group, as well as his address and a contact.
- Always tell someone where you are going and when you are likely to be back.
- Especially on longer rides, try not to go alone. Two or three people is much safer and usually more enjoyable!

Safety on the Hills
Though Derbyshire and the Peak District are generally low level compared with 'real' mountainous areas we would advise reading of the B.M.C.'s booklet 'Safety on Mountains'. A lot of the information from this book may be relevant, especially in winter or early spring in the northern areas of the Peak.

WEATHER
Be prepared for very changeable weather on the higher routes, especially the Edale, Glossop, Gradbach and Hayfield circles. Generally the most useful weather forecasts are local ones such as daily forecasts displayed at one of the Peak Park information centres or one of the recorded message type regional forecasts available by phone.

ALLOWING TIME
The times mentioned at the beginning of each route should only be used as a very rough guide. They were mainly estimated by riders (who ride daily) of medium fitness, in good weather when ground conditions were firm. You are probably the best person to judge your own riding speed or that of the slowest rider in your group.

Always allow more time than seems necessary so a puncture or long dinner stop doesn't mean you get caught out in the dark. Bad weather, especially rain, wind, snow and ice and very soft surfaces can literally double or triple the time you would normally take to ride an off-road stretch.

Remember the more people you have in your group the more potential there is for accidents, punctures and mechanical breakdowns. All these, and other extra variables mean you need to allow more time. More people = allow more 'spare' time.

General Equipment

MAP AND COMPASS

Along with this guidebook we strongly recommend carrying the appropriate large scale map of the area in which you are to ride. The appropriate map or maps are specified at the beginning of every route. Equally important (providing you can use it in conjunction with the map) is an accurate Silva type compass. There may be times on some routes when a compass proves invaluable especially if you manage to get off course. Learn how to use one properly through regular practice!

WHISTLE

A whistle is useful for attracting attention and summoning help in real emergencies on the hills. The international distress signal is six long blasts followed by a minute gap before repeating.

FOOD

Cycling, especially off-road, consumes calories at a vast rate. Therefore it is wise to carry plenty of food containing sugars easily broken down by the body to replenish energy losses quickly. Replace fluids that are lost by having plenty to drink both before and during the ride. Adequate fluid intake also helps prevent cramp.

CLOTHING

Personal preferences and wallets will dictate what clothes you wear for off-road biking. You may find most racing/touring clothes too insubstantial or over-engineered for off-road riding. A number of layers is probably best. It allows you to regulate your temperature by stripping off, or putting more on as necessary. Depending on the season it's very important to have gloves, hat, waterproofs and spare jumpers with you. On the higher routes always carry a waterproof and spare jumper with you whatever the season. Some people consider 'colour pollution' to be a problem in the countryside.Give this a thought when purchasing clothing.

HELMET

A helmet ought to be high on your list of sensible equipment to buy. Shop around for one which is comfortable, fits well, allows good airflow and conforms to ANSI and SNELL Institute safety standards or has a British Kite Mark. Then use it! Take good care of it when it is not being worn, especially the soft shell type.

YOUR BIKE

Riding Technique and Maintenance

We are not going to try and cover which type of bike you should have, and how to maintain it. These subjects are well covered in other specialist books, or better still picked up from other people.

However it is important that your bike is always safe and ready to ride. Wash and maintain your bike regularly paying careful attention to brakes and tyres. Be aware of the limitations of your particular bike (and of yourself) and ride well within them.

If you thrash your bike and/or don't have a good riding technique, expect lots of expensive and frustrating breakages. The best way to prolong the life of your bike and its parts is to learn how to ride it properly; gain the skills that minimise the amount of abuse it has to take.

Remember you can always get off and walk!

Always ride with care. Remember:

A - It only takes the smallest of tree roots to unseat the biggest and best of riders!

B - Irresponsible riding can seriously injure others as well as yourself.

WASHING YOUR BIKE - Washing your bike prolongs the life of gear parts and chains and ensures they can work properly. Washing also enables you to have a close look at each part of your bike so that you are more likely to spot, for example, the head tube which is about to part company with the down tube, the misaligned brakes or the inner tube about to escape from a split in your tyre.

VIBES FROM YOUR VELO - Learn to listen to your bicycle for creaks, rattles or squeaks. Feel the play in, (for example) a loose headset or crank while riding and respond with appropriate maintenance before the ailment develops into a major problem.

LIGHTS AND REFLECTORS

Front and rear lights and a red rear reflector are required by law after dusk. As well as lights, reflective strips are a big aid to being seen. At dusk they may even prove more visible than your lights. If you sew them onto clothing or equipment do it strategically. Basically be safe, be seen!

TOOLS AND SPARES

Whether your bike is an old, well-used hybrid of mis-matched parts or a brand new machine displaying the latest gleaming Italian or Japanese group-set, it is going to let you down some time. A sensible tool kit to carry for most bikes would be: A pump, spare inner tube, puncture repair kit, 4, 5, 6mm Allen keys, a small screwdriver, a chain riveting tool, a spoke key and an 8/10mm spanner or adjustable spanner. For longer trips oil, spare spokes, zip ties, PVC tape, spare nuts and bolts and other specific tools may be useful.

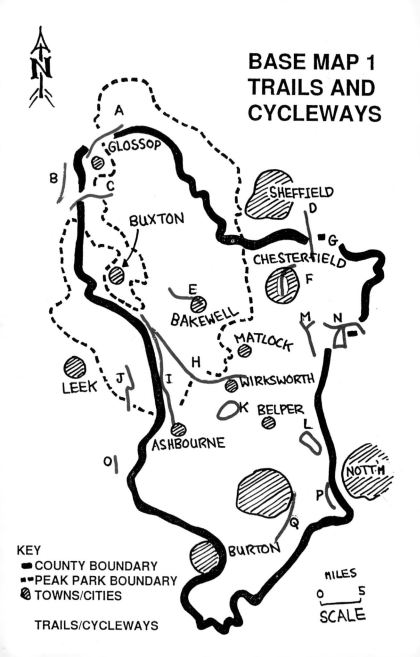

**BASE MAP 1
TRAILS AND
CYCLEWAYS**

N

A

GLOSSOP

B

C

BUXTON

SHEFFIELD

D

G

CHESTERFIELD

F

E

BAKEWELL

M

N

MATLOCK

H

LEEK

J

I

WIRKSWORTH

K

BELPER

L

ASHBOURNE

O

P

NOTT'M

Q

BURTON

KEY
■ COUNTY BOUNDARY
▪▪ PEAK PARK BOUNDARY
▨ TOWNS/CITIES

TRAILS/CYCLEWAYS

MILES
0   5
SCALE

BASE MAP 1

TRAILS AND CYCLEWAYS IN DERBYSHIRE AND THE PEAK DISTRICT

A	Longdendale Trail
B	Middlewood Way
C	Sett Valley Trail
D	Rother Valley Country Park
E	Monsal Trail
F	Chesterfield Canal
G	Beighton to Staveley Trail
H	High Peak Trail
I	Tissington Trail
J	Manifold Light Railway
K	Carsington Reservoir
L	Shipley Country Park
M	Five Pits Trail
N	The Pleasley Trails
O	Churnet Valley
P	Long Eaton to Heanor Cycle Route
Q	Derby Cycleway

TRAILS AND CYCLEWAYS IN DERBYSHIRE AND THE PEAK DISTRICT

(see Base Map 1. Page 18)

KEY   For asterisked locations
CP   Carparking
PS   Picnic site tables
T   Toilets (not necessarily always open)
I   Information Centres (not necessarily open)
CH   Cycle Hire (not necessarily open)
Bao   Bridleway access only, (accessible by bike but not by car)

SETT VALLEY TRAIL (Hayfield)

Map: O.S 1:25 000 Outdoor Leisure: 1-Dark Peak

The Sett Valley Trail is a two and a half mile length of old railway track (built for the Midland and Great Central Joint Railway Company, opened 1868) running between Hayfield and New Mills. Bought by Derbyshire County Council in 1973 three years after it closed, it now offers a traffic-free route for walkers, horse-riders and cyclists. D.C.C. produce a good leaflet on the trail.

The line used to serve the many water-powered spinning mills along the Sett Valley as well as carrying coal, raw materials, goods from paper mills and large numbers of passengers (to and from Manchester). The hilly scenery is dramatic. There is lots to see including the Torrs Gorge. The trail is linked with the surrounding countryside by a good network of footpaths and bridleways.

The trail is not a public right of way. Its use is at D.C.C. discretion and subject to users obeying the bye-laws displayed on the back of information signs.

The trail can be joined by bike at:
- Hayfield Station (CP,PS,T, I,CH)   SK 036869
- Ravensleach, Hayfield Rd. (Bao)   SK 019867
- High Hill Rd., New Mills (Bao)   SK 009865
- Torr Top (CP,I)   SK 001854

MONSAL TRAIL

Map: O.S. 1:25 000 Outdoor Leisure:
24-White Peak (east and west)

The Monsal Trail uses part of the former Midlands Railway line closed by British Rail in 1965 and bought by The Peak Park in 1980. This line ran from Matlock to Buxton. Peak Rail Operations Ltd. aim to re-open this line as a Standard Gauge Light Railway, to run both steam and diesel trains on. Presently they have got permission for and have actually laid line on, the stretch between Matlock and Darley Dale.

This trail runs between Coombs Viaduct near Bakewell and Topley Pike (Wye Dale/Chee Dale) SK 112726. However cycles are only allowed on the stretch between Coombs Viaduct and SK 194712, the end of the blocked tunnel which, if open, would lead onto Monsal viaduct. The rest of the trail, a mixture of ex-railway and footpath links, is for walkers only. If you have left your bike at home it is well worth walking since it passes through some splendid limestone dales such as Miller's Dale, Chee Dale and Wye Dale.

SECTION FOR CYCLING - The section you can cycle on is a very pleasant three and a half miles of flat, hard cinder track, edged with young silver birch and other trees. You can join the trail on a bike at:

- Coombs Viaduct   SK 217705
- Bakewell Station (CP)   SK 223690
- Hassop Station (CP)   SK 217705
- You cannot leave or join the trail by bike at SK 194712, near Monsal Tunnel since there is only a footpath link with Little Longstone.

FIVE PITS TRAIL

(Grassmoor Country Park, near Chesterfield, to Tibshelf Colliery)
Map: O.S. 1:25 000 Pathfinder:
779 Mansfield (North)/Sherwood Forest SK 46/56

This trail, a seven and a half mile traffic-free route for cyclists as well as walkers and horse-riders, uses the disused railway lines surrounding the collieries (also now closed) in this area of north-east Derbyshire.

It runs from Grassmore Country Park, more or less due south to the site of Tibshelf Colliery, and is very easily accessible from Chesterfield or the M1. The mineral railways once served five large busy coal pits. As the coal seams were worked out the collieries were closed. By 1973, when all the collieries were closed, the railways also became redundant, (at least for their original purpose). Derbyshire County Council has used the derelict land, not just for these trails but as reclaimed land for forestry, agriculture and industry.

D.C.C. produce a good leaflet on the trail, which isn't just a straight track but has several loops. It is basically re-claimed spoil heaps; a landscape which has not matured much yet but has potential as a haven for wildlife and already has the huge advantage of being away from traffic. The cycling is easy going on hard tracks but is not completely flat.

HIGH PEAK TRAIL

Map   O.S. 1:25 000 Outdoor Leisure:
            24-White Peak (east and west)

The High Peak Trail is a seventeen and a half mile (28km) stretch of old railway track with a cinder surface that is firm in any weather. This traffic-free trail was converted by Derbyshire County Council and the Peak Park Planning Board (with Countryside Commission help) for use by walkers, cyclists and horse-riders. It uses the track of 'The Cromford and High Peak Railway' (closed 1967). The railway was an important link in the canal network joining the Cromford and Peak Forest (Whaley Bridge) Canals. One of this country's earliest railways, it was built in the 1830s at a cost of £180,000. The engineers toyed with the idea of building a canal but difficulties such as long slopes and the lack of water on the limestone upland meant a railway was more feasible. However they still used canal building principles. Locks were replaced by steep inclines with a steam-powered beam engine at the top of each one, to pull the wagons uphill. The line transported coal, iron and minerals.

Today it's a very interesting and well-used trail through varied Derbyshire countryside. There are engine-houses, crags, old quarries and villages along the route. Good leaflets on the trail are available from the Peak Park and Derbyshire County Council. The trail can be joined at:

* High Peak Junction, Cromford Canal   SK 313560
* Black Rocks (CP,PS,T)   SK 294557
* Sheep Pastures Incline (Bao)   SK 304561
* Middleton Top (CP,PS,T,I,CH)   SK 276552
* Near Hopton Works (Bao)   SK 252546
* Longcliffe Station   SK 225557
* Minninglow (near Pikehall, CP,PS)   SK 194581
* Newhaven Crossing (A5012)   SK 180597
* Friden (CP,PS)   SK 172607
* Parsley Hay (CP,PS,T,I,CH)   SK 147636
* Hurdlow/Sparklow (CP,PS)   SK 127660
* The end of the trail is Dowlow (near Buxton)   SK 111673

The High Peak Trail is joined by the Tissington Trail just south of Parsley Hay.

The High Peak Trail is almost completely flat (there is in fact a very slight slope downhill from Buxton) except for three notable exceptions, all uphill towards Buxton:

1. Sheep Pastures incline - From High Peak Junction at Cromford Canal SK 313560, a consistently steep climb of more than half a mile to SK 300561.
2. Middleton Incline - Roughly 700 metres, again very steep. From SK 282551 to Middleton Top SK 276552.
3. Hopton Incline - Hardly worth noting, much easier than the other two, SK 258546 to SK 250547.

Highly recommended; easy riding but it can get very busy in summer, especially at weekends.

TISSINGTON TRAIL (Ashbourne to Parsley Hay)

Maps: O.S. 1:25 000 Outdoor Leisure: 24-White Peak (east and west)
Pathfinder 810 Ashbourne and Churnet Valley Sheet 04/14

The thirteen mile (21km) Tissington Trail is in many ways similar to the High Peak Trail though it pre-dates it as a traffic-free path (opened in 1970). It runs from Ashbourne (CP,PS,CH) SK 176469 to join the High Peak Trail at SK 147633 near Parsley Hay. Again it is almost completely flat (there is a **very** slight downhill slope from the Parsley Hay end) and has a good surface. The verges support a large number of wild flowers/plants as do those of the High Peak Trail. There are generally wide vistas but some stretches pass through deep cuttings too. Cyclists can also join this trail at:

• Spend Lane   SK 174484
• Fenny Bentley (CP,PS)   SK 166503
• Tissington (CP,PS,T)   SK 178521
• Stonepit Plantation (CP,PS)   SK 156549
• Biggin   SK 161592
• Hartington Station (CP,PS,T)   SK 149610

Leaflets on the Tissington Trail are produced by both D.C.C. and the Peak Park.

MANIFOLD WAY (Manifold Light Railway, Hulme End near Hartington, to Waterhouses)

Map: O.S. 1:25 000 Outdoor Leisure:
24-White Peak (east and west)

The Manifold Way (Light Railway, 1902-1934) runs from Hulme End to Waterhouses following the River Manifold for 6 miles and the River Hamps for the final two. The smooth tarmac track curls between some startling scenery. There is an old copper mine at Ecton, Thor's Cave towers 250 feet above the valley floor, Beeston Tor has been a favourite with climbers for nearly a century and in the widening valley at Wettonmill there are contorted rock outcrops with a medieval feel. Here too there is a café and camping site at the National Trust owned farm.

The River Manifold disappears down swallow holes at Wettonmill except in wet weather. The dry river bed has boulders and the huge leafed butterburr. Hazel, ash and hawthorn provide a haunt for a mass of bird life including woodpeckers, wagtails, nuthatch, blackcap and long-tailed tits.

Cyclists can join the trail at:

• Hulme End (CP)	SK 103593
• Ecton Bridge (CP lay-by)	SK 091577
• Wettonmill (CP, PS, café, camping)	SK 095561
• Weag's Bridge (CP)	SK 100542
• Waterhouses (A523 T road)	SK 091501
• Waterhouses (CP,PS,CH)	SK 086501

Most of the Manifold Way is free from cars which is partly why it is so popular. However the stretch between Ecton SK 096583 and just south of Wettonmill SK 098556 uses a public road. A nice alternative to the road (for cyclists) is to use the gated road which runs from Ecton Bridge to Wettonmill on the east side of the river.

The Manifold Way is very popular with walkers and cyclists (cycle hire at Waterhouses) and so in summer or on fine week-ends it can get very busy.

SHIPLEY COUNTRY PARK

Map: O.S. 1:25 000 Pathfinder:
812 Nottingham (North)/Ilkeston sheet SK 44/54

Shipley Country Park (near Heanor) has a number of cycle routes varying in length between two and six miles. There is also a picnic site, visitors' centre, toilets and cycle hire at Coppiceside carpark, the north west edge of the park, SK 432454. The landscape varies. There is farmland and reclaimed coal pits but also several fine lakes and some much older woods with beech, silver birch, oak, hazel, hawthorn and many other trees. Hedges form the boundaries rather than walls. The paths are generally well surfaced. Do not cycle on the footpaths. There is a leaflet produced by D.C.C. showing the cycle routes. Worth a visit!

DERBY RECREATION ROUTES

Map: O.S. 1:25 000 Pathfinder
852 Burton on Trent sheet SK 22/32
832 Derby and Etwall sheet SK 23/33

Sustrans are developing a whole network of paths in and around the Derby area. You can ride from Derby city centre to:
Melbourne
Elvaston Castle

Little Eaton
and   Sinfin Moor Lane

The paths are surfaced and well waymarked using riverside paths, old canals, disused railway lines and quiet roads. Leaflets are available from Sustrans and Derby City Council.

The path from Derby city centre is a useful six-mile link to Swarkstone Lock (Trent and Mersey Canal) SK 372292 and the two Ticknall routes.

- To join Ticknall/Robin Wood Circle at Stanton by Bridge (Alternative Start/Finish point A, SK 373272):

(Adds a further two miles each way).

From Swarkestone Lock cross the canal, ride straight along the track, passing under the railway to meet the A5132. Turn right onto the road and follow it as it curves ninety degrees left, crosses the river Trent and then Swarkestone Bridge. After the bridge is a short rise. Take the first road right into the village of Stanton by Bridge. You can start and finish the Ticknall/ Robin Wood Circle from here.

- To Kings Newton:

(Adds a further three miles each way). From Swarkestone Lock cross the canal, ride along the track, under the railway to the A5132. Turn left then next right signposted 'Weston upon Trent, Aston upon Trent, Melbourne Cycleway'. After roughly three quarters of a mile, just before a railway bridge (Weston Road SK 386284) cross the road to take the narrow path beside the railings, signposted 'Melbourne Cycleway'. Ride along the old railway for three quarters of a mile until, just after a ranger's hut, a tarmac drive forks right and leads up to a small road (Trent Lane, Kings Newton) SK 390266. Take this, turn right onto the road then right again into Kings Newton.

- To Ticknall:

From the Packhorse pub in Kings Newton continue along the road. Take the next left signposted 'Melbourne' (Derby Road B587). Do not go into Melbourne centre, but follow the B587 as it curves right. After three quarters of a mile go right on the road signposted 'Ticknall'.

NEW TRAILS

CARSINGTON WATER

Map: O.S. 1:25 000 Outdoor Leisure: 24-White Peak

This recently created reservoir near Wirksworth has a circular ride of 7 to 8 miles around its edge, the majority of which is off road. The visitor centre (SK 240518) has a wide range of facilities including a restaurant bar and a variety of shops. There is also a sailing club and water sports base. Can be very busy at weekends.

TRANS-PENNINE TRAIL

A proposed recreational route from coast to coast linking the Mersey and the Humber. Possibly also forming part of the European Long Distance footpath eventually connecting to Istanbul! A few sections are currently available to cyclists in Derbyshire and the Peak District.

LONGDENDALE TRAIL

Map: O.S. 1: 25 000 Outdoor Leisure: 1 - Dark Peak

An old railway track bed between Hadfield and Woodhead running beside Woodhead Reservoirs which has been converted for the use of walkers, cyclists and horse riders. See the Glossop ride which now makes use of this traffic free route. A leaflet is available from North West Water.

BEIGHTON STAVELEY TRAIL

Map: O.S. 1:50 000 Landranger 120

Not yet officially open but ridable. Another disused railway track.

CHESTERFIELD CANAL

Map: O.S. 1:50 000 Landranger 119

A canal towpath from the centre of Chesterfield eventually linking to the Staveley Beighton Trail. It should be ridable in 1997.

THE PLEASLEY TRAILS

Map: O.S. 1:50 000 Landranger 120/ 1:25 000 Pathfinder 779

Three trails on the Derbyshire, Nottinghamshire border west of Mansfield. The trains follow disused railway lines which once linked the area's coal pits to nearby towns and industries. The Teversal Trail and Meden Trail can be used by cyclists. There is a visitor centre on Canarvon Street, Teversal (SK 479613).

CHURNET VALLEY

Map: O.S. 1:50 000 Landranger 128

Three miles of off-road cycling on a disused railway track bed between Alton and Denstone.

MIDDLEWOOD WAY

Map: O.S. 1:50 000 Landranger 118 and 109/
1:25 000 Outdoor Leisure: 1-Dark Peak

The track bed of the former Macclesfield, Bollington and Marple railway on the edge of the Peak District. Eleven miles have been converted for recreational use between Macclesfield and Marple.

LONG EATON TO HEANOR CYCLE ROUTE

Map: O.S. 1:50 000 Landranger 129

Erewash Borough Council are promoting a traffic-free path from Long Eaton town centre to Shipley Park and Heanor. Started in 1993, it has now been completed as far as Stanton Iron Works.

ROTHER VALLEY COUNTRY PARK

Map: O.S. 1:50 000 Landranger 120

The country park lies to the south east of Sheffield (SK 452820). It has a wide range of recreational facilities including four miles of off-road cycling.

Salters Lane
Clough Woods

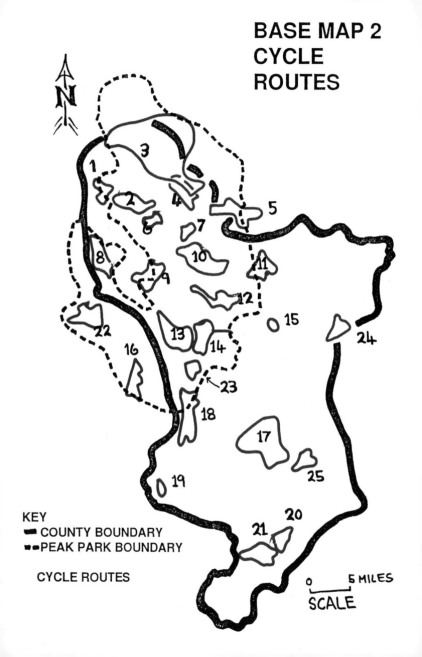

BASE MAP 2
CYCLE
ROUTES

N

1
3
2
4
5
7
8
10
11
8
1 9
12
22
13
15
16
14
23
18
17
24
19
25
20
21

KEY
━━ COUNTY BOUNDARY
▪▪ PEAK PARK BOUNDARY

CYCLE ROUTES

0   5 MILES
SCALE

BASE MAP 2

CIRCULAR CYCLE ROUTES IN DERBYSHIRE AND THE PEAK DISTRICT

1 Hayfield
2 Edale
3 Glossop
4 Ladybower
5 Stanage
6 Castleton
7 Bradwell
8 Buxton
9 Chelmorton
10 Baslow
11 Linacre
12 Chatsworth
13 Middleton-by-Youlgreave
14 Darley Bridge
15 Ashover
16 Manifold
17 Derby North
18 Ashbourne
19 Doveridge
20 Ticknall/Robin Wood
21 Ticknall/Repton Shrubs
22 Gradbach
23 Minninglow
24 Bolsover
25 Locko Park

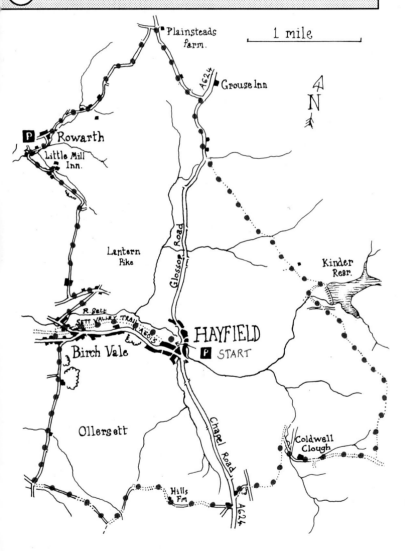

Plainsteads farm.

1 mile

A624

Grouse Inn

N

P Rowarth

Little Mill Inn.

Lantern Pike

Kinder Resr.

Glossop Road

R Sett

SETT VALLEY TRAIL

A6015

Birch Vale

HAYFIELD

P START

Ollersett

Chapel Road

Coldwell Clough

Hills Fm

A624

HAYFIELD

Hayfield, Sett Valley Trail, Peep-O-Day, Coldwell Clough, Kinderlow End, Kinder Reservoir, Middle Moor, Plainsteads, Rowarth, Sett Valley Trail, Hayfield Circle.

DISTANCE: 16 miles/26km (3mls/5km on road)
TIME: 4 hours
MAPS: O.S. 1:25 000 Outdoor Leisure: 1-Dark Peak

A compact route strenuous even for the fit rider, but highly rewarding for its fine views of the west side of Kinder plateau and the moorland areas that surround Hayfield. Do not forget to take your O.S. map with you on this ride; you will need it.

Start in Hayfield at the Sett Valley Trail carpark SK 036869. Follow the trail west for a good three quarters of a mile, then turn left onto a small path (bridleway) next to a stile and large gate, opposite the end of the reservoir. On meeting the A6015, turn right towards New Mills, but after only 250 metres take the first road left. Climb steadily on tarmac for about a mile, passing Birch Vale Quarries as you go. The tarmac deteriorates by Moor Lodge (buildings on the left). Continue uphill for about 500 metres ignoring the track which breaks off to the left (Piece Farm). Soon after the track levels, you should come to a junction. Laneside Road drops right. You should turn left on the bridleway.

You will soon go through a large gate, continuing uphill on the obvious track. The next mile of bridleway follows this walled lane onto, then across the moors.

Three quarters of a mile from the start of this walled lane, having passed through two more large gates, you should come to a junction of paths. There will be a piece of open moorland (without walls) in front of you. Turn left on the bridleway just above the wall and follow this rather boggy stretch of track. After about 600 metres, just before Foxholes Clough is a junction of paths (with a fingerpost). The bridleway left drops back into Hayfield. You should go straight on across the moor following the right-hand wall.

You will soon be riding along a walled lane again, pass through several gateways and drop steeply to Hills Farm. Your bridleway goes through the farm's garden so please walk through quietly and shut the gate. Continue descending then ride along a flat but wet section, past Hills House to join the A624.

Go left but after only 100 metres turn right onto a track between a house and barn. It passes an old quarry then meets a large gravel track. Go almost straight across this track through the bridlegate and follow the left-hand wall along the path to the second wooden five-bar gate. Passing through

Tim climbing out of Hayfield

this and dropping diagonally left the rutted path takes you to a road. Turn right, ride downhill to cross the stream and go through a gate before climbing up the road. Pass a farm at Coldwell Clough dated 1804.

Shortly after this the surface becomes gravel. One track curves sharply right, a second goes straight on, more steeply uphill. Take the latter. About 400 metres up this hill (some walking may be needed) you should come to a point where a path crosses yours and there is a wooden four-way fingerpost. Continue straight on up to and through the next gate. There will be another gate immediately on your left. Ignore this but after a further 100 metres turn left by passing through a large gate onto moorland.

Have a look at your O.S. map now. You are now on the bridleway heading towards Kinder Reservoir. Follow the more or less flat path (a bridleway that is not very distinct on the ground) for about 150 metres and cross a sandy footpath. After a further 150 metres you will join a better path. Bear left onto this better path then follow it until you see a large wooden five-bar gate (the right-hand one) with **stile and stone gateposts** below Kinderlow End. Go through this gate, follow the bridleway as it bends left along a narrow walled section to a boundary post and large gate. Go left through this gate onto Hill House Estate.

To your right are good views of Kinder Downfall. Ride more or less straight on, on the obvious green path across a field to a small gate with stone posts. Continue down the next two fields and pass through a large gate onto a track beside the edge of the wood. Follow this stony farm track to a small road just below Kinder Reservoir.

Cross the road, go straight down the path, cross another service road then turn right to climb the steep zigzag bridleway onto Middle Moor. At first it is cobbled. At the first junction/corner (opposite the start of the reservoir) turn acutely left and continue uphill. After a small open gateway bear left again. At the top, by a fingerpost and footpath, turn left.On meeting a track with a green metal sign go straight across. The white shooting cabin should be to your right. You will cross a boggy section on a new wooden bridge then ride between the heather on a fine sandy path. This path fords a stream, continues for roughly half a mile then descends to ford a second stream before joining the A624 at Carr Meadow.

Turn right uphill. After half a mile take the first left signposted 'Charlesworth'. After about three quarters of a mile take the first proper tarmac road left (marked dead end, and in a due west direction). Turn left again after only 100 metres, opposite the footpath sign. An enjoyable, fairly flat tarmac stretch followed by a long descent will take you to a house and gate. Continue along a muddy, walled track overhung by large beech trees to ford a small stream then climb uphill to a small road. Turn left and descend into Rowarth.

At the houses in Rowarth take the first left by Anderton House ('No Motor Vehicles Except For Access'). Pass a telephone box then go through the small gate with bridleway fingerpost just right of 'The White House'. There is a short bumpy section before you are on tarmac again. Curve left in front of the Little Mill Inn. There is a dead end sign. The road forks just before Laneside Farm. Ignoring the left, go straight on. You should now be on a rock-strewn track steeply uphill and initially more or less unrideable.

Pass a disused quarry to gain a flatter, sandy section of track before climbing again. Ignore a track left. Ride down the bumpy track past a farm with dogs (luckily most on leads) to join a road. Go left. Five hundred metres down the hill is a row of cottages on your left. Turn right on the bridleway opposite. On the first sharp bend left, go through the small bridlegate straight on to descend the much narrower path. It is very bumpy but soon comes to a road. Turn left then after about 200 metres left again through a bridlegate and onto the Sett Valley Trail. Follow the trail back to your starting point.

*2002 At the start follow the trail west to Station Road, turn left up the road to meet the A6015

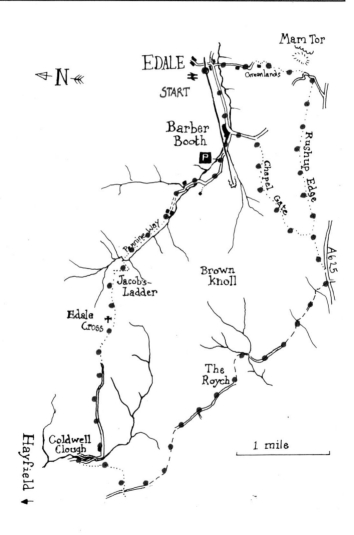

◁ N ◁

Mam Tor

EDALE

START

Greenlands

Barber
Booth

P

Chapel Gate

Rushup Edge

A 625

Pennine Way

Brown
knoll

Jacob's-
Ladder

Edale
Cross

The
Roych

Coldwell
Clough

Hayfield ◀

1 mile

EDALE

Edale, Barber Booth, Upper Booth, Jacob's Ladder, Coldwell Clough, Mount Famine, Roych Clough, Chapel Gate or Rushup Edge and Cold Side, Edale Circle.

DISTANCE: 14 miles/22^1/$_2$km (3mls/5km on road)
                      Rushup Edge option 17mls/27km
TIME: 4^1/$_2$ hours
MAPS: O.S. 1:25 000 Outdoor Leisure: 1-Dark Peak

Edale is one of the few routes in this book to be almost entirely off-road. It uses some of the ancient pack-horse routes that criss-cross the Peak. This tough route has roughly 2538ft. (780 metres) of climbing. The surfaces are generally very rutted and rocky. Most people would need to do a fair amount of walking on this route. It is quite a high level route with demanding terrain and changeable weather so equip yourself accordingly. Not recommended for inexperienced riders.

Start at the carpark almost opposite Edale Station (trains from both Sheffield and Manchester stop here) SK 124853 or at the parking lay-bys between Barber and Upper Booth SK 107847. From the Edale carpark head right on the road towards Barber Booth. After nearly three quarters of a mile you will cross the River Noe and then should turn immediately right to follow the road signposted 'Upper Booth'.

It passes under the railway and past the parking lay-bys mentioned earlier in the text. Roughly half a mile of tarmac should bring you to a five-bar gate with a National Trust sign saying 'Lee Farm'. Go through the gate, up through Lee Farm, climbing gently to the bottom of Jacob's Ladder on a sandy/stony track.

On reaching Jacob's Ladder, ford the stream (or cross via the small but impressive packhorse bridge) before tackling the very steep zigzag path left. The bottom section is rideable, at least in part. You will see the steps of the even steeper footpath to your right. Jacob's Ladder is very heavily used; as a route up on to Kinder Scout generally, and to join the Pennine Way. The path is very rocky, steep and has suffered badly from erosion but has been stone pitched and drainage improved. Some walking will no doubt be needed.

When at the top you meet a five-bar gate, you will probably want a rest, or have already had about four. Push on through the gate on a short sandy stretch of badly rutted track till you reach the top of the hump. Go through an empty stone gateway. A medieval monument, Edale Cross, should be immediately on your right.

There is now a very rough rocky descent which should be tackled with caution. About a mile should take you to another wooden gate. Pass through it still on a rough track, but over a grass field rather than moorland. Continue

downhill past a fingerpost then onto a gravel track to a gate. Go through this and join the smooth tarmac road. Bliss! You are now at Coldwell Clough. The stream, a tributary of the River Sett, should be to your left. Pass a farm dated 1804 on your right and ride down to where the road forks and there are two gates. Pass through the left-hand gate.

Follow the road a short way uphill. Turn next left onto a waymarked bridleway climbing diagonally up the hill for about 300 metres (doubling back on the road slightly) then when the track forks curve gently right (do not cross the small stream to your left) to a large gate. Go through this gate then follow the wall and fenced bridleway to meet a larger track.

Turn left. Follow this rocky walled track for 400 metres, initially straight on and then as it curves left slightly to meet two gates, one large and one small, across the track in front of you. There is moorland beyond the gate and a distinctive Peak Park sign nearby. Go through the gate to follow the rutted resemblance of a track straight on, following the line of the right-hand wall.

It is less than half a mile to the next gate. The sandy rutted track can be wet with large puddles. After the gate, if the weather allows, there is a good view of Chapel-en-le-Frith to your right.

You curve round below South Head and will be able to see Coldwell Clough to your left. Ignore the footpaths left and tackle the steep rocky section of track ahead that is banked high on either side. What follows is three quarters of a mile of rough descent. A short distance after the next gate a track joins yours from the right (a possible foul weather escape route?). When you reach a choice of two gates side by side, choose the left before the drop into Roych Clough begins in earnest.

At the bottom, ford two streams before climbing again. The next half a mile section is rough (as if it hadn't been already!) and will involve some walking.

Follow the gated track that thinks it is a stream bed. Soon there is a smoother stretch. Cross the small stream at Bolehill Clough, curve right, pass Tom Moor Plantation and ride on to meet the A625 road from Chapel. Turn left, then left again after only 50 metres onto the gated bridleway/unclassified road. This leads onto Rushup Edge.

You are now about an hour or less away from your starting point in Edale. Nearly half a mile up this very badly eroded track with large rock steps (some walking) you come to a large gate followed by a cairn and signpost. On the other side of this gate are two options A and B:

(A) - Turn left and follow the very steep bridleway known as Chapel Gate. It curves right at first. Ignore a small path which forks left by a wooden post and continue to follow the more distinct track. Drop downhill with care, pass through gates as necessary and continue until you meet a road. Turn

Edale Cross

left downhill back to Barber Booth and then your starting point, at Edale or Upper Booth parking lay-by.

Or:

(B) - Go straight on up to and along Rushup Edge (splendid views in clear weather). At first the track follows just left of the wall. However after about a third of a mile there should be a small wooden gate in this right-hand wall. Go through this gate, off the well defined path which becomes a footpath, onto a poorly defined bridleway, and almost immediately through a large gate.

This goes along parallel to the wall on moorland but on the **right-hand (south) side**. If you come to stiles and locked gates you have obviously missed the small gate and need to backtrack to find it. On the correct path you should reach a metal five-bar gate. Go through this, drop downhill to a smaller wooden gate then meet the road.

At the road turn left and cycle just over the brow. From here either follow the road steeply downhill to Barber Booth or turn right on the bridleway (a small gate shortly after the highest point of the road ie almost immediately). In fact two bridleways run from this gate.

Take the left-hand one which descends to Hardenclough Farm and then Edale. Again it is sandy and eroded by water but all rideable and good fun. It will bring you out on the road between Barber Booth and Edale, very close to your starting point.

Doctor's Gate Path, Glossop Circle

N

A628

Crowden

P

Woodhead Resr

LONGDENDALE

Bleaklow

Devils Elbow

B6105

Doctors Gate

START

GLOSSOP

A57

Featherbed Top

Snake Inn.

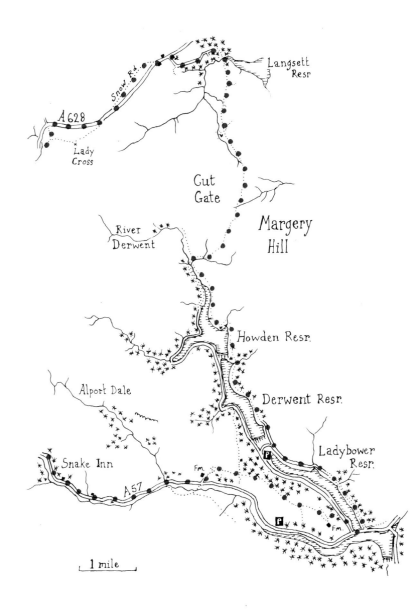

GLOSSOP

Glossop, Woodhead Reservoir, Longside Edge, Lady Shaw, Snow Road, Milton Lodge, Swinden Lane, Mickleden Edge, Cut Gate, Ladybower Reservoir, Bridge-end Pasture, Snake Road, Doctor's Gate, Glossop Circle.

DISTANCE: 38 miles/60km (14mls/26km on road)
TIME: 8 hours
MAPS: O.S. 1:25 000 Outdoor Leisure: 1-Dark Peak

Glossop circle is the longest and probably toughest route in this book. It is, however, very rewarding with a real variety of terrain and views, and a high moorland feel. Its height, length and rough ground conditions mean it is vital to go properly equipped and allow lots of time. It took us about 8 hours in very dry, fine conditions. It begins with road and straightforward hard-packed track then tends to get rougher as you progress. The route involves roughly 3400 ft. (1040 metres) of climbing and some difficult 'technical' (or walking!) sections.

Start in Glossop on the B6105 (Woodhead Road), which passes the railway station, SK 035941. The ride starts by climbing out of Glossop in a northerly direction. Pass Cemetery Road on your left (signposted Padfield) then three quarters of a mile further on choose the next left, Padfield Main Road. Turn next right immediately after passing between two small reservoirs. A pleasant downhill with sharp corners drops you to a bridge over the Longdendale Trail. Only 200 metres past this look for the waymarked bridlegate and path on your right onto the trail. Turn left and follow the trail for an easy two miles to cross the B6105 and then a further four flat miles to the blocked Woodhead Tunnel.

As you leave the trail (to your right) you will briefly re-join tarmac but should then take the track left uphill to cross the busy A628 road with care. Walk up the new path (with steps) opposite onto Pikenaze Moor to join a larger track near Audenshaw Clough. Turn right. The track alternates between firm grass and hard-packed stone/sand or a mixture of the two but stays dry in most conditions. After passing through another gateway the track climbs and dips, traversing Longside Edge before joining the road again roughly two and a half miles from where you left it.

Cross the road with care and go through the small gap in the crash barriers opposite. Drop down the track to cross Salter's Brook by a narrow stone bridge before climbing straight on, alongside Ladyshaw Dike. Where the track curves left follow it north across the moor to meet the A628 opposite a road junction.

Turn right and follow the road for a good mile. At the top of the hill you should be able to see a triangulation point on your left. Shortly after this go left on the marked byway next to a road sign warning motorists of sheep. It leaves the road at an acute angle to pass through a wooden five-bar gate. This 'Snow Road' is a grassy track through a mass of young heather and bilberry plants. It is rutted, just over a mile in length and all downhill until you re-meet the road.

Turn left onto the road but after 500 metres go right down a waymarked track (bridleway) beside Delmont Garage. Go through a metal five-bar gate and descend for roughly 200 metres. Look out for a fingerpost left to a large gate. If you pass this, go left at the sharp right-hand corner which will bring you to the same gate onto Swinden Lane.

Follow this walled lane, with a grass and hard-packed surface slightly downhill, passing through three gateways. At the fourth take a left turn down a farm track towards coniferous woodland. On forking you want the left-hand, grassier of the two tracks into Crookland Wood (the right-hand track is a footpath up past an old derelict farm). Turn right after 400 metres. Enjoy a brief smooth gravel section then drop steeply out of the woods to cross Brook House Bridge.

Begin climbing the small sandy path onto Delf Edge. You will soon be up on real moorland; Hingcliff Common. The track's surface varies. It is mainly of sand and rock but there are also peaty sections. When you see a track veering left (in a south-easterly direction) ignore it. Continue straight on until you drop down slightly to Haslingshaw before beginning a long climb up the left-hand side of Mickleden Beck.

From the open access boundary (for walkers not you!), shown on the ground by a wooden post with sign, it is a generous mile and a half to Howden Edge. Howden Edge, at 530 metres, is the high point before you begin descending. On the way up to Howden Edge, the first mile is a steady climb on a loose rock/sand path. It is almost all rideable with a lot of effort, but soon the nature of the path changes. It becomes less steep and has an uneven, softer, stepped surface with rocks, peat and groughs. In wet weather this section could be very hard going with large boggy areas needing a lot of walking. When dry it is virtually all rideable. Follow the obvious path straight on; do not go left down any groughs by mistake!

Now for some fun! You drop off the moors still on the Cut Gate path into Cranberry Clough, losing about 250 metres of height. The descent has a real variety of surfaces. Smooth peat and sand at the top gives way to rocks and large (dangerous) drop-offs at the bottom. You will need to get off and walk short stretches here. Take care!

Ford the stream at the bottom. Continue along to where a path from your right merges with yours. This is the footpath from Howden Moor. Go left crossing the very small wooden bridge over a stream. In front of you should be a stone packhorse bridge.

Curve left onto a wide, 'forestry type' track with a very compact 'fast' surface. Follow it slightly downhill for about four miles skirting the east edge of Howden and Derwent Reservoirs. Just below Derwent Reservoir you will meet a tarmac road. Do not turn right to cross under the dam wall but continue straight on passing Jubilee Cottages and a telephone box.

About a mile of tarmac road leads to a well-surfaced track. Follow this for a mile and a half to the Ashopton Viaduct (A57 road). Turn right to cross the viaduct then immediately right again. Cross the cattle grid and stay on the road for less than 600 metres before turning left to follow the very steep bridleway to, and through, Crookhill Farm.

You will probably need to do some walking here. Go through the farmyard via two gates keeping to the right. Join the track onto Crook Hill, following the right-hand wall (ignoring tracks that fork left uphill) until you come to a gate. Go through the gate and follow the wall for about 150 metres before bearing left slightly to cross open grassland (following the wooden waymarked posts). Head for the large gate. Go through this and up the field to a bridlegate. After this there is a flatter section, following wooden stakes. You should get panoramic views of Castleton, Edale and other places from this point.

On reaching another bridlegate pass through it before descending over grass to the edge of the woodland. Follow the edge of the wood to a junction of paths with several gates. You should go straight on following the 'Bridleway to Rowlee' sign.

This sand and grass track takes you about half a mile to a fingerpost and cross-junction of bridleways. Go straight on then down the good gravel farm track. A very steep gravelly section with Z-bends takes you past Rowlee Farm to join the A57 Snake Road. Turn right.

Now follows a four and a half mile slog passing the Snake Inn about half way up. When you seem to be getting near the top, on one of the corners, keep an eye out for a lay-by and National Trust sign on the right-hand side of the road. It will say 'Doctor's Gate' and will be beside a bridlegate. Turn right here.

You are only about four and a half miles from Glossop but this last section took us about an hour and a half. It is difficult terrain involving a lot of dismounting/re-mounting and some walking too. Drop down to and cross a stream. Follow the sketchy path (eroded) up from the stream and across the moors. The first half mile, to the point where you cross the Pennine Way, is hard going with some boggy peat sections.

Follow the old Roman road; you may be able to see some of the cobbled remains. You will come to a point where the descent starts. It is not unlike the drop-offs and terrain back at Cut Gate but is more fearsome. Take great care over the next two or three miles. Dismount and walk as necessary to avoid injury! From beside Rose Clough there is a mile of rocky track where you can only ride a short way before having to get off and walk a section then get back on. It is very tiring.

You will cross Shelf Brook on a small wooden footbridge and continue along to the 'Open Access' boundary. Here go left onto a smoother, rideable track. Continue downhill until you meet a large metal gate. After passing through this gate you should be able to see Mossy Lea Farm on your left. Cross the small **right-hand bridge** and follow the track straight on, through a number of gates, past some mills and back into Glossop. Well done!

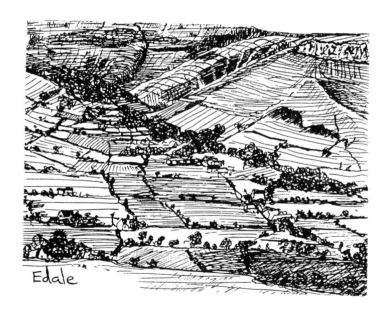

Edale

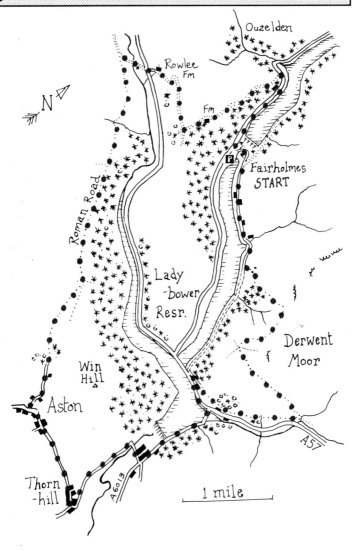

Ouzelden

Rowlee Fm

Fm

N

Roman Road

Fairholmes START

P

Lady -bower Resr.

Derwent Moor

Win Hill

Aston

Thorn -hill

A6013

A57

1 mile

LADYBOWER

Ladybower Reservoir, Lockerbrook Farm, Rowlee Farm, Roman Road, Aston, Thornhill, Derwent Moor, Derwent, Ladybower Circle.

DISTANCE: 18 miles/29km (6mls/10km on road)
TIME: $4^1/2$ hours
MAPS: O.S. 1:25 000: Outdoor Leisure: 1-Dark Peak
                  Pathfinder 743 Sheffield sheet SK 28/38

This hilly ride, a large circle including sections of the moors surrounding Ladybower and Derwent reservoirs, should give a taste of the 'High Peak' landscape. Though not quite as high or bleak as the nearby Glossop, Hayfield or Edale circles, this circular route should be very satisfying for most riders. A range of tracks, paths and roads, many of which were ancient pack-horse routes, take you over farmland and gritstone moorland, through both conifer plantations and broadleaf woodland. There are good hilltop vantage points over the surrounding scenery.

Start SK 173893 at Fairholmes picnic site and carpark, just below the dam wall of Derwent Reservoir. Turn right out of the carpark onto the tarmac road and follow it up the west side of Derwent Reservoir for roughly three quarters of a mile. After passing Gores Farm on your left you will curve round a left-hand corner. Just as you begin to descend take the bridleway left, signposted 'Bridleway to Snake Road 2 miles'.

Climb up this steep but mostly rideable track into a conifer plantation. Well used by mountain bikes, its surface is a mixture of stones embedded in sand and pine needles. It is generally firm but does have some puddles and mud patches.

The track becomes less steep further up, then starts to descend slightly. As you pass Lockerbrook Farm watch out for black rabbits. Cross the stream and go through the gate before climbing a short distance up a wider track. Less than quarter of a mile after the farm you should come to a point where the track forks, one half curving round to the right while the other descends left.

Choose the right-hand option and cycle down the well-surfaced gravel farm track to a very steep section with Z-bends. You should come to Rowlee Farm.

From here go straight across the A57 Snake Pass road and downhill on the small tarmacked road marked with a dead-end sign. Cross over the River Ashop then climb uphill to, and through, a large gate. About 300 metres after this gate take the first left turn, a track leaving the road at an acute angle. You will have a steady climb of about half a mile on a compact rubble-type surface before dropping down to pass through a gateway and ford at Blackley Clough.

Go along to the next gate. From here the track is downhill on a rutted grass surface with some mud. Go straight on through the next two gates. Just after the second gate is a stone guide post, 'Hope Cross'. Follow the ridge to another large gate. After this gate the track forks. You should bear left slightly, on the semi-defined path which rises gently towards the edge of the conifer plantation.

Follow this path parallel to the wood's edge, along the ridge for about three quarters of a mile. You should come to a semi-derelict wall with a gateway and single stone gatepost. Only 300 metres after this look carefully for a small turn-off right. There may be a small cairn by it but it is not very well defined on the ground. Follow this grassy track downhill, through a gate below Top Plantation before forking slightly right.

At the four-way fingerpost go straight on, cycling across a field (do not turn right down into the woods), then into a 'funnelling' of walls which takes you into a walled lane. Pass through two gates. After the second you will come to a tarmac drive and Edge Farm. Curve right and descend to meet a road at a T-junction.

Turn left. Follow this rather shady embanked lane for roughly a mile. Pass through the village of Aston ignoring all turns off until you come to a T-junction at Thornhill. Go left following the sign 'Ladybower 2¹/₂ miles'. There is a good downhill stretch before the road curves right to cross the River Derwent, then a very short climb to the A6013 where you should turn left.

On meeting the A57 go left again. After no more than half a mile turn right, just before Ashopton Viaduct, on the road marked 'No Parking, No Vehicles'. Curve immediately right (do not go through the bridlegate straight ahead of you) and climb uphill past a number of houses. The surface becomes gravelly. Pass through a wooden five-bar gate. Very soon you will come to a hair-pin corner left but go straight on through the large gate.

You should be on a smooth grass path which climbs gently then drops to a gate. After this gate drop down to a T-junction with another track. Go left uphill then pass through a gate with a sign saying 'Ladybower Wood Nature Reserve'. Continue riding along to cross a stream and come to another gate. After this gate you will be on a pleasant narrow moorland track amongst heather.

Above Cut Throat Bridge (just before a stream clough) the track forks. Take the left option onto the moors and away from the road. On meeting another track turn left again. Climb up onto Derwent Moor. Cycle for roughly a mile to a cross junction of paths at Whinstone Lee Tor. Turn right on the waymarked bridleway, slightly downhill. This path, with some boggy patches, traverses the moor just above a gritstone wall.

After about half a mile, at the top of Grainfoot Clough, there should be a metal sign pointing out Derwent left and Moscar right. From here turn left through the gate and descend to a bridlegate. Go through the gate and

Riding down towards Rowlee Farm

continue down the path as it follows the right-hand edge of the plantation. Drop down to a ford.

After the ford the bridleway goes through a large gate between two very old small barns. Turn left through a narrow gateway onto a very steep grass hill. Follow the path down until you meet a hard track beside the reservoir.

Turn right onto this track. Ride along the east edge of the reservoir. You will curve left and cross Mill Brook then soon reach a small tarmac road. About three quarters of a mile along this you will come to a telephone box and Jubilee Cottages. Just past this point keep following the tarmac road (rather than the track) which curves left below the wall of Derwent Dam back to your starting point.

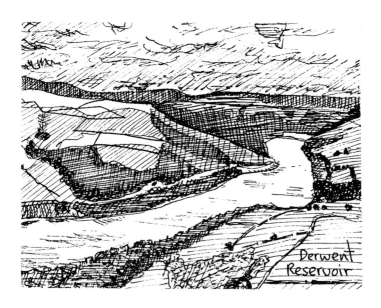

Fording the stream Blacka Plantation, Stanage

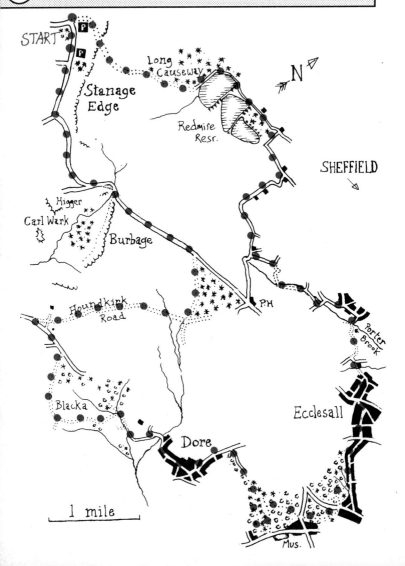

START

P
P

Stanage
Edge

Long
Causeway

Redmire
Resr.

N

SHEFFIELD

Higger
Carl Wark

Burbage

Houndkirk
Road

PH

Porter
Brook

Blacka

Ecclesall

Dore

Mus.

1 mile

STANAGE

Long Causeway, Stanage Edge, Ecclesall, Ecclesall Wood, Dore, Blacka Plantation, Houndkirk Road, Burbage Moor, Dennis Knoll, Long Causeway Circle.

DISTANCE: 23 miles/37km (11½mls/18km on road)
TIME: 5 hours
MAPS: O.S. 1:25 000 Pathfinder 743 - Sheffield sheet SK 28/38

This ride starts on the moors north of Hathersage, below the imposing Stanage Edge, a long gritstone escarpment usually speckled with climbers and walkers. Then it passes over moorland and touches the outskirts of Sheffield passing through suburban housing and mixed woodland. Climbing away from Sheffield, back into the Peak, the route again crosses moorland on well-compacted paths before a road stretch below Stanage Edge brings you back to the finish.

Start SK 227843 by Dennis Knoll. Ride northwards up the rough track that leaves the road at the sharp corner after a cattle grid. This track, the 'Long Causeway', climbs about a mile to Stanage Pole. It is mainly a rock-strewn sand track so although often wet it should not be too muddy. It curves onto the edge, follows the top a short way then curves east-wards to a high point of 438 metres (above sea level) at Stanedge Pole.

From here ride down the rutted bumpy track towards Redmire Reservoirs passing through the gate part-way down. Turn left at the bottom of the hill onto Redmires Road and follow this round the north side of the reservoirs.

From here you will be able to see the city of Sheffield sprawled below you. After less than half a mile of descent, as you begin to climb again take the first road right; Brown Hills Lane. Take the next right by Peat Farm. This road zigzags steeply uphill then levels before dropping downhill. You want the third road left, about a mile from Peat Farm, called Greenhouse Lane (keep an eye out for a pebble-dashed house on your left and, immediately after it, a small road left; the third turn, which you want, is only twenty metres further.

Five hundred metres down Greenhouse Lane the road bends ninety degrees left. You should leave the tarmac here by continuing straight on. This waymarked by-way, Clough Lane, descends steeply to cross a footpath and then Porter Brook. You should follow the brook for a short distance then re-cross it and join a small tarmac road.

Ignoring the road left go straight on to the next T-junction where you should turn left. You will cross the brook again, curve right and start climbing. Ignore the road that joins you from your left. You are on Mayfield Road. At the next junction, a small cross-roads, turn right and ride downhill. After

Ecclesall Wood

only 250 metres the road curves sharply left. However you should turn right beside Brook Lodge on the road marked as a dead-end.

After dropping downhill ignore a bridleway left. Cross the brook, take the next waymarked bridleway left (just after the footpath beside the brook). This climbs to Whiteley Wood Road. Turn left onto the road but then take the first right after only 100 metres, onto the waymarked by-way just above the farm. Ford the stream and ride up the track into a residential area.

You will be on Trap Lane and should follow it along, ignoring any turn-offs, until you meet a larger road just opposite Bents Green Methodist Church. From here turn right, then immediately left, onto Knowle Lane (which is the road just below the church). Take the first right turn onto Harley Road. Ride down here, straight across the next two crossroads onto Dobcroft Road

After roughly 750 metres you should see signs for school children crossing and a road, both on your left. Immediately opposite this is a signposted bridleway between two houses which is very difficult to see. Turn right off the road down this bridleway into a very pleasant mixed wood with large deciduous trees, mainly oak, sycamore and beech.

This is Ecclesall Wood, which has a number of footpaths and bridleways. Follow the instructions carefully, use your O.S. map and keep to the more defined paths. Follow the blue arrow and bridleway sign, cross two streams and, when the path forks, go left. You will soon meet a road and should go straight across to re-enter the wood on the lower of the two paths. On meeting a second road go almost straight across, using not the stile but the wooden gate below it. When the track forks bear left. About 500 metres should bring you to another junction.

Turn left almost back on yourself and ride downhill. When this path splits into about four options take one of the left-hand paths directly down to Abbeydale Road which should be visible below you. You should come out on the road opposite the end of the millpond (there is a museum, open to the public on certain days, called Abbeydale Industrial Museum, on the far side of the road). Do not cross the road but go back into the woods uphill on the bridleway signposted 'Dore'.

It may be difficult to distinguish your path but stick to the most substantial path which curves left, skirts up inside the left-hand edge of the wood and crosses Limb Brook. You will probably see hundreds of squirrels.

After crossing the brook turn right, still following the signs 'Bridleway to Dore'. The path climbs slightly uphill through an area dominated by Scots pine. Go up the stretch of walled lane to a road called Limb Lane. Go left here towards Townhead, continuing on the road until you meet a road junction, (a slightly offset cross-roads). Go straight across onto High Street then first right opposite the Hare and Hounds pub. You are on Townhead Road. This is a good spot for dinner with a pub, shops and a fine chip shop!

After refreshment head up the road through the residential area before descending steeply to cross Redcar Brook. About a hundred metres after this turn left onto Shorts Lane, waymarked as a bridleway. Ride down this hard compacted track curving sharply right at the bottom, to follow 'Bridleway to Blacka Moor' signs. Continue descending and fork right to follow the signs rather than crossing the stream.

After a stone gateway is a large board with a map of the bridleways in Blacka Moor Plantation. Ride on up the main track until it splits just before another gateway with stone pillars. Bear left to ford the stream then climb steadily up the narrow path.

It is a good path through mixed woodland (mainly oak, elder, alder and birch) with noisy streams nearby. Some walking will probably be needed. You go off the Pathfinder map here very briefly but don't panic. On meeting a T-junction of bridleways turn right uphill. This rough track goes through a gate, climbs over rough grassland and passes between two stone gate pillars. Continue up here through another gate and along the compacted track to join the busy Hathersage Road. Turn left onto the road.

Ignore the road off left to Calver and Bakewell. About 500 metres down the hill you will see a track right signposted 'Parson House Farm'. Do not take this but take the next right soon after it which leaves the road at an acute angle.

This undulating sand and rock track is Houndkirk Road which crosses Burbage and Houndkirk moors. After 200 metres go straight over the farm track and through a gate. Follow the good track for about a mile and a half. You will cross Sparkinson's Spring then, after another 400 metres you will drop slightly into a second stream clough. At this point another track crosses yours. Turn left.

(If you come to the edge of the plantation and a wooden five-bar gate before turning left you have missed the turning so go back slightly). The left-hand turn also takes you to the plantation edge but to the west edge which it follows all the way to Ringinglow Road.

Go left onto the road and ride about a mile and a half, passing over Upper Burbage Bridge (Higger Tor, Carl Wark and Burbage Edge are all down to your left), before taking the road right signposted 'Ladybower 6'. An enjoyable downhill follows but you want the first right at the bottom so do not overshoot. This road takes you along below Stanage Edge.

Go right again at the signpost 'Ladybower 4'. A mile and a half of road will take you back to your starting point.

*2002 last paragraph on p.53 should read ' Ignore the road left, ride straight on, then take a signed bridleway left. After 100 metres cross the road, go through the bridle gate and follow the well-surfaced path. Soon rejoin tarmac by some large stone houses. Turn right, then immediately right again on the signed bridleway that climbs to Whiteley Wood Road.'

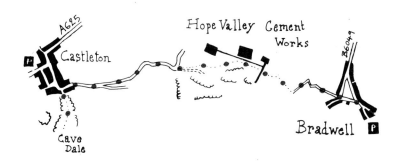

CASTLETON CIRCLE/BRADWELL CIRCLE LINK

The start/finish points of the Castleton and Bradwell circular routes are less than two miles apart. These rides combine well to make a good day's ride. We would suggest starting with the Castleton Circle then doing the Bradwell Circle before finishing back in Castleton.

From the end of the Castleton Circle to the start/finish point of the Bradwell Circle:

When you emerge from Cave Dale and meet the small road in Castleton, turn right. After 400 metres, when the road forks, go left. Nearly half a mile along this undulating road is a sharp left-hand corner. Turn right here off the road, through a small gate and onto a waymarked bridleway just below a large track. This good bridleway is well waymarked and will take you straight through Hope Valley cement works. Beware of large lorries and other machinery.

Roughly half a mile along here, after a short but steep climb you will meet a farm track and should turn left. Descend the walled path to meet a road junction in Bradwell. Go straight across the small road and down Town Lane to meet the B6049. Turn right and the carpark start point for the Bradwell Circle is about 300 metres along here on your left.

From the end of the Bradwell Circle to the start-finish of the Castleton Circle:

After dropping down from Bradwell Edge, turn right onto the B6049. Ride back into Bradwell for 500 metres before turning left up Town Lane. At the top of this lane go straight across the small road and follow the walled path uphill for roughly 400 metres. Turn right onto the waymarked bridleway signposted 'Castleton' and follow this all the way through Hope Valley cement works to meet a road.

At the road turn left uphill. About half a mile will bring you to a junction where you have to give way. Turn right and follow this road back into Castleton. Curve right to pass the Youth Hostel and join the A625 in Castleton. Turn left back to your Castleton Circle start/finish point.

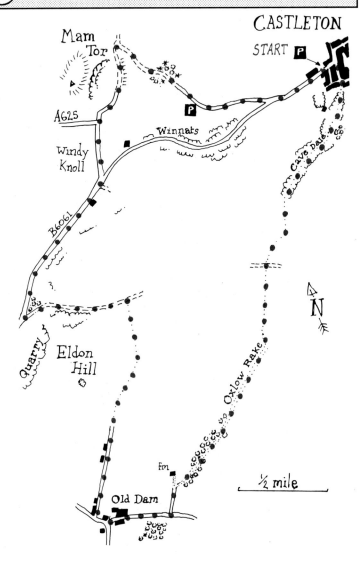

CASTLETON

START

Mam Tor

A625

Windy Knoll

Winnats

B6061

Cave Dale

N

Quarry

Eldon Hill

Oxlow Rake

Fm

½ mile

Old Dam

CASTLETON

Mam Tor, Windy Knoll, Eldon Hill Quarry, Old Dam, Oxlow Rake, Cave Dale, Castleton Circle.

DISTANCE: 9 miles/14^1/$_2$km (3mls/5km on road)
TIME: 2 hours
MAPS: O.S. 1:25 000 Outdoor Leisure maps:
1-Dark Peak, 24-White Peak (west)

This short ride is mainly well drained and easy going, on roads, hard tracks and grass, with a final fun descent down a narrow rocky limestone dale. It would make a pleasant summer's evening ride. If you wanted to make a day or two's trip, the Castleton area has plenty of other off-road rides to try as well as attractions such as show caves, good climbing and walking, pubs and cafés. But be warned, it is a favourite tourist spot.

Start SK 149829 at the carpark in Castleton. Leave the carpark and turn right up the road. When the Winnats Pass road forks left, you should curve right on the old Mam Tor road. This passes the entrance to Treak Cliff Cavern and a lay-by which could offer an alternative starting point.

Go through the gate by Odin Mine. Follow the old subsiding road beneath Mam Tor (avoiding the tarmac crevasses) to join the B6061. This dramatic start feels rather like riding in a country suffering from earthquakes.

From here follow the Sparrowpit signs, along the road. You want the first bridleway left after a mile and a quarter, just before the ever-expanding Eldon Hill Quarry. This sharp left takes you back along a stone track past both the quarry and a large gate on your right. Almost at the top of the hill turn right (due south) through a large gate with railway sleeper gate posts onto a bridleway across a field.

The bridleway almost follows the left-hand wall as it contours round the tumulus (ancient burial mound) then drops to join a farm track at another gate. Ride down the farm track past the farm. Turn left and then left again which should take you up Old Dam Lane. After 500 metres of gentle climbing on tarmac turn next left. This leads to Oxlow End and takes you beside a farm. Turn right through the gate onto Oxlow Rake and climb up the track through the woods.

Follow the track with Oxlow Rake (depressions, humps and bumps) to your left until, roughly a mile from where you joined this track below the woods, while heading downhill, you come to another gate. Another bridleway from Starvehouse Mine joins yours from the right. Bear left to cross over the rake. Follow the left-hand field edge to a junction of tracks with a number of gates.

Choose the bridleway to Castleton (which is straight on). It goes across

Riding down Cave Dale

fields to Cave Dale. After 600 metres a footpath which looks the more substantial of the two choices forks left and heads very slightly uphill but you should bear right through a narrow metal gate. Win Hill, a conical hill a few miles away, should be visible straight ahead of you in clear weather.

After the second small gate the fun starts with a very technical rocky downhill section which should test both your wheels and your trials skills. Anything from a dozen or so judicious dabs with one foot to a stretch of walking may be needed here. Once through the pleasant steep-sided Cave Dale (note, this bridleway is heavily used by walkers) you are soon back in Castleton. You will emerge on a small road.

There is an option of a link with the Bradwell Circle from here, see link instructions, page 57).

Riding down the road then turning left should bring you back to your starting point.

Mam Tor, Castleton Circle

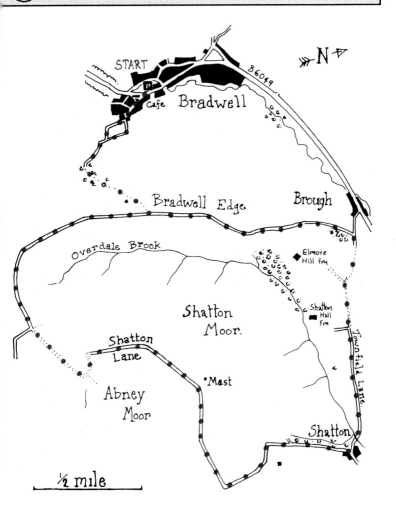

START

Bradwell

Cafe

B6049

Bradwell Edge

Brough

Overdale Brook

Elmore Hill Fm

Shatton Moor.

Shatton Hall Fm

Shatton Lane

Townfield Lane

•Mast

Abney Moor

Shatton

½ mile

BRADWELL

Bradwell Edge, Shatton Lane, Shatton, Brough, Bradwell Edge, Bradwell Circle.

DISTANCE: 6 miles/9¹/₂km (1ml/1¹/₂km on road)
TIME: 2 hours
MAPS: O.S. 1:25 000 Outdoor Leisure: 1-Dark Peak

This is another short ride in the Castleton, Hope area. A stiff climb takes you up onto Bradwell Edge where there is open moorland and great views of the surrounding area. It is not unusual to see hang-gliders or hard winged gliders (from the nearby Great Hucklow gliding club) overhead. A circle of the moors on well-drained wide tracks with fast descents and short, steep climbs will bring you back to this edge. Then you return to Bradwell down the path you laboured up initially.

Start SK 174813 at the public, Parish carpark in Bradwell, next to the 'SPAR' foodstore. Turn left out of the carpark onto the B6049, pass the church on your left and you will soon see the Valley Lodge public house to your right. Opposite this pub is a small road off left. Take this left turn. Ahead of you some pedestrian steps should be visible. Follow the road as it curves right, then dog-legs back left to reach the top of these steps. You are about to start a very steep but short climb of roughly half a mile to Bradwell Edge.

There are cottages on your left and soon a road forks off uphill to the right. Ignore it and follow Bessie Lane as it drops into a dip.

Ignoring the second fork right, climb up out of the dip. You should now be at a point with a fingerpost and two options, left or right. The right fork is tarmac road, the left goes to a field gateway where you should bear right up a narrow overgrown path. (They meet higher up the hill where the surface becomes loose gravel.)

The path between scrub soon becomes narrow. As you go through the small wooden gate beside a stile you will notice it is becoming very steep. Some walking will no doubt be in order. The path at first follows the right-hand fence then winds its way up the hill. One consolation is you will later be riding **down** here. When the path forks, take the bridleway left just above a gritstone wall. The next section is rideable, so continue following the old wall up to Bradwell Edge.

On meeting another fence/wall at the top of the ridge curve abruptly right and follow this wall along the top of the hill for roughly 100 metres to a small metal gate on your left. Go through this gate, cross the field and turn right onto the gravel track. This track sweeps round in a large gentle left-hand curve above the head of Over Dale.

After about a mile you should come to a junction where a road to the right drops down to Abney and a footpath goes off left. Carry straight on

along the RUPP which is a grassy but still wide track signposted 'Bridleway to Shatton 2 miles'.

After roughly quarter of a mile curve left at the point where another fingerpost says 'Bridleway to Shatton' and a footpath leaves to the right. Soon you curve right, join a walled track and go through a gate onto Shatton Lane. You have now got a mile and a half of steep downhill to come but care should be taken since there is a loose gravel surface and a gate part way down. To your left slightly, in the distance you may be able to see the bottom of Ladybower Reservoir.

Go past the large TV/Radio mast on your left, down to and through the gate, **opening it first!** There is a sharp corner left, then the road drops very steeply. Take the first road left by Wheat Hay Farm, ride through the ford and follow Townfield Lane towards Brough.

After half a mile the road disappears and drive forks left to Shatton Hall Farm (Upper Shatton on O.S. map). Fork right on the good track, along the left edge of one field. Ignore a second track left to Elmore Hill Farm, go straight on through the gate and down the short steep descent to join a road on a hairpin corner.

Turn left and climb uphill. The surface soon becomes stony. Continue up this stiff climb for about three quarters of a mile, until you are at the point where you joined this track from Bradwell Edge earlier in the ride. Look for the metal gate on your right just after a track drops gently to the left. Turn right through the large gate, go across to, and through the small metal gate.

Follow the bridleway (you struggled up earlier) down into Bradwell. Take care on the steep descent. Finish at the pub for sustenance.

*2002 The Spar is now a Co-op!

Noel climbing onto Bradwell Edge

BUXTON CIRCLE

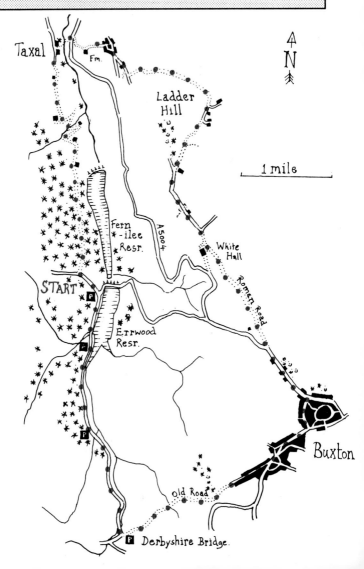

BUXTON

Errwood Reservoir, Goyt's Clough, Derbyshire Bridge, Macclesfield Road, Buxton, Roman Road, Ladder Hill, Taxal, Hoo Moor, Errwood Reservoir Circle.

DISTANCE: 15 miles/24km (6mls/10km on road)
TIME: 3 hours
MAPS: O.S. 1:25 000 Outdoor Leisure: 24-White Peak (west)

This hilly route starts in the Goyt valley. It skirts Buxton and sweeps in a large circle back to Taxal and then through Hoo Moor plantation to the reservoirs. There can be a few boggy patches but generally surfaces are suitable for most weather conditions. On a clear day there are fine views from the hilltops, both of Kidner to the east and over the Cheshire Plain to the west.

We started this route from the carpark at Errwood Reservoir SK 102748 although other possible starting points would be: Buxton, Whaley Bridge or the picnic site close to Derbyshire Bridge.

Assuming you start at Errwood, turn right out of the carpark and begin the long steady climb up the road towards Derbyshire Bridge. There are rewarding views over Goyt's Moss, Burbage Edge and into Goyt's Clough. After passing over the tiny Derbyshire Bridge you will approach the carpark and picnic site. Turn left off the narrow road and continue climbing on a compacted track signposted 'Path 6 to Berry Clough', keeping the carpark to your right.

This well-surfaced track is the old Macclesfield road. It will take you across open moorland. Climb roughly half a mile to the high point of the route then descend into the Burbage area of Buxton, passing through a gate as you do so (with the old High Peak railway to your left).

Back on tarmac, you soon join the A53 Leek road at the main cross-roads by Christchurch. Turn left onto the A53. Freewheel about half a mile down into Buxton and as the hill flattens out slightly take the left-hand turn signposted 'Cavendish Golf Course' (Carlisle Road). Climb up this road to meet a T-junction. Turn left here, then on meeting the very busy A5004 Whaley Bridge road turn left again. Climb away from Buxton for roughly half a mile. After passing Cold Springs Farm on your left the road bends sharply to the left. Leave the road here, by crossing with great care to fork right on a track which technically is almost 'straight on'. This narrow roadway was once a Roman road linking Buxton with more northerly towns and forts.

Climbing steeply at first, the track takes you over typical Peak moorland. It's an upland grazing area so do not forget to close gates behind you. After this climb you then descend past Whitehall Outdoor Centre and mountain rescue post following the track as it curves to the right. Continue straight on, ignoring the road that drops right towards Combs, and you should find yourself climbing up the tarmac road towards the natural gap in the ridge at Wainstones. From here, as you descend, take the first right forking off the road at Wythen Lache Farm. Go through the gate and into a walled lane which can be muddy.

After the second gateway the track crosses open fields and is badly rutted. It will take you quickly down to another narrow tarmac road above Thorny Lee. Turn left and drop down the steep hill with caution. At the sharp right-hand bend in the road turn left into a walled lane. Climb up and traverse around Ladder Hill (on top of which is a TV mast). The steep stony track soon levels out. The surface becomes sandy and there are excellent views north over Chapel, with Kinder Scout forming the horizon.

Drop downhill on this rough track. At the next road junction turn right and ride down past Elnor Lane Farm. Turn right at the first T-junction and go down the road. Take the second road left by houses, a telephone box and post box. This should be Shallcross Road. Ride to the end of this road. It narrows to a single-track road bounded by trees before reaching Shallcross Hall Farm. Fork right down a steep rutted track which will deposit you on the A5004 just outside Whaley Bridge.

Cross with care into the large lay-by opposite. Roughly halfway along this lay-by is an opening in the wall which leads onto a steep track into the wood. Take this, dog-leg round the corner and ford the River Goyt at the bottom, (riders without webbed feet can use the bridge). A very steep, but thankfully short climb takes you between the graveyards of St. James Church into Taxal.

At the top of this climb turn left along the narrow road, mostly uphill to Overton Hall Farm. At the farm turn left. The track drops steeply, bends and twists down to the stream passing a small farm on the way. Cross the stream in Mill Clough. Climb up the path away from the stream for 250 metres. Just before Knipe Farm, on the brow you should head off right, through a gate in the wire fence onto grass fields. Still uphill, the path across the fields stays close to the left-hand edge (bounded by a plantation). Pass through the next gate and dog-leg left up the walled bridleway. Go through a gate to pass barns and a stable, keeping to the lower of two tracks. Cycle along to another gateway and Oldfield Farm. Pass quietly through the farmyard, then take the upper track leading into Forestry Commission woodland, waymarked 'Hoo Moor'.

The next mile is strenuous gravel track but you are not far from the end of the ride now. At the end of the wood, where you meet a tarmac road, turn left and enjoy a very fine smooth downhill. Curve right at the bottom to follow the edge of Errwood reservoir back to your starting point.

Near Buxton

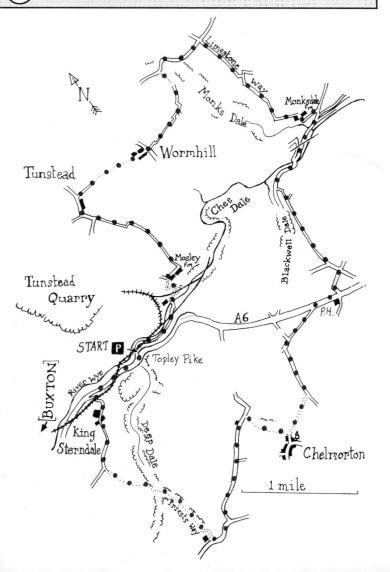

N

Limestone way

Monks Dale

Monksdale

Wormhill

Tunstead

Chee Dale

Blackwell Dale

Mosley Fm

Tunstead
Quarry

A6

P.H.

START P

Topley Pike

River Wye

BUXTON

Deep Dale

King
Sterndale

Chelmorton

1 mile

Priests Way

CHELMORTON

Topley Pike, Wye Dale, King Sterndale, Horseshoe Dale, Chelmorton, Limestone Way, Miller's Dale, Limestone Way, Wormhill, Wye Dale Circle.

DISTANCE: 15 miles/24km (3^1/$_2$mls/5^1/$_2$km on road)
TIME: 3^1/$_2$ hours
MAPS: O.S. 1:25 000 Outdoor Leisure: 24-White Peak (west)

A real variety both of surfaces and scenery is offered by this ride. There are steep-sided scenic limestone dales, gravel tracks, green roads, muddy bridleways, stretches of walled lanes (the 'Limestone Way') and complex patterns of walled fields around Chelmorton. The high ground can be a little exposed if it's windy. Some sections of this route are muddy so perhaps avoid it in very wet weather. There are plenty of ups and downs and a little walking so allow yourself plenty of time. A deceptively tough ride for its length especially in wet weather.

Start in the Monsal Trail carpark off the main A6 Buxton, Bakewell road (opposite Topley Pike quarry entrance) SK 104725. This can get very busy especially at weekends as it is a popular carpark for the northern end of the Monsal Trail. Turn right onto the A6. Follow it for roughly half a mile then go left on a track marked 'Unsuitable for Motors' (opposite a stone bridge across the river). It heads diagonally back up a steep hill at an acute angle to the road.

This rideable gravel track curves right, flattens out and enters King Sterndale by a stone cross and the village green. After another half mile the now tarmacked road curves right, but we take the waymarked track straight on, through a small wood (Horsestone Hill Plantation) and gate onto grass fields. Do not follow the footpath which hugs the wall to your right. Instead go through the gate and across the field diagonally on an undefined path, aiming for a gate slightly to the right of the fence dividing the two lower fields.

Cross the next field diagonally too. You will see a small gate. Go through this rather than the five-bar gate and you will be in an area of rough tussocky grass. There is a steep drop on one side of you into Deep Dale so take care. Ride a short way parallel to, but above, the dale before dropping down the path which has a sharp left-hand bend at the bottom. Go through the gate in front of you and follow 'Priest's Way' up the small but attractive Horseshoe Dale. There are some tricky mud and rock areas around the gateways. After passing through a farm, you should join the A5270.

Go left and follow the undulating road for nearly a mile, ignoring the two right turns to Chelmorton. Further up this road, at the top of a rise, you will see the end of two stone houses (Arden Villas) on your left. Two hundred

metres past these, on your right, go through the second gate just next to a drystone wall.

This is an undefined grass bridleway which you follow as it contours round under Chelmorton Low, just above the limestone wall. After one field go through another large gate. Keep following the right-hand wall. This section can be very muddy. Walk if necessary. You will reach a small bridlegate in the right-hand wall below a large sycamore tree. Go through this; Chelmorton Church will now be straight in front of you and the Church Inn just below you. Turn left and climb up the track which soon levels out.

You will ride along a rake, over slag from the old open-mine workings. On meeting a bridlegate turn **left** onto a wide gravel track. Follow this for 400 metres. Go through a large gate then ride down the rutted track. After another large gate turn right, then shortly, when the track turns left, go straight on following Senners Lane along to the A6. Turn right, then take a left turn opposite the Waterloo Hotel down Priestcliffe Road.

At the next cross-roads turn left. Then as the road curves left, watching carefully for traffic, take the track straight on. This is the Limestone Way. It is a steep descent. Watch out for potholes and walkers. On meeting the road turn right down to Miller's Dale. Ignore the first road left (uphill to Miller's Dale café) and continue along the road under the huge steel railway bridges. After a church take the small but very steep road uphill to the left. After less than 150 metres turn left again on the bridleway (Limestone Way) into the woods then left through Monksdale Farm.

Follow this walled lane which can be muddy. After about three quarters of a mile, at the fork, turn left. Ride along the walled lane to a road and Monksdale House. Turn left. A steep downhill and sharp bend are followed by more uphill. Pass a footpath on your left. Less than 150 metres from the bottom of the hill go left through the large metal gate onto an undefined bridleway, up and across the field aiming for the top left-hand corner. At the top of the field is a small gate into a walled lane. Follow this uphill. After a small gate take the right fork. At the next junction go right again through a large gate and continue along the walled lane.

On meeting the road at Wormhill turn right then immediately left, up through Old Hall Farm. Pass through the farm yard bearing slightly left to pass through a large gate (normally open) onto a stony track. Follow this along the left-hand side of a wall. Drop downhill, then go through the right-hand gate following the path with a wall to your left to the road and turn left. Go past some quarry houses and take the right fork signposted 'Concessionary Bridleway'. When the road curves right take the bridleway left, a pleasant green track.

On reaching Mosley Farm turn right above the buildings, then go left down a zigzag grass track which drops dramatically into Chee Dale. Waah! watch you don't over-shoot any corners! Cross the river in front of a row of

Limestone Way

houses, by ford or foot bridge and then turn upstream. Follow the track parallel to the river (do not ride on the old railway line) about half a mile back to the carpark you started at.

*2002 After the Quarry Houses follow the signed Concessionary Bridleway to Mosley farm

Silly Dale path, Baslow Circle

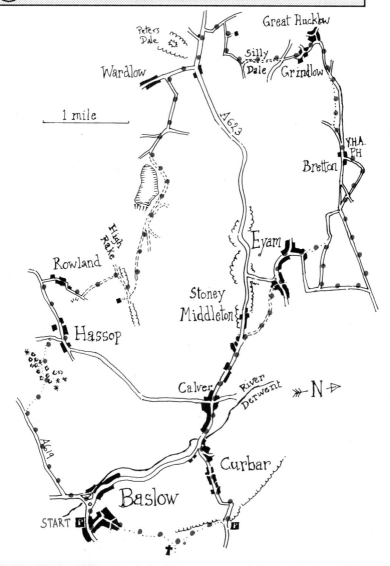

Peters Dale

Great Huckow

Silly Dale

Grindlow

Wardlow

1 mile

A623

Y.H.A.
P.H

Bretton

High Rake

Rowland

Eyam

Stoney Middleton

Hassop

Calver

River Derwent

≫ N ▷

Curbar

Baslow

A619

START

BASLOW

Baslow, Hassop, Rowland, High Rake, Wardlow Mires, Grindlow, Great Hucklow, Eyam, Stoney Middleton,Calver, Baslow Edge, Baslow Circle.

DISTANCE: 22 miles/35km (10mls/16km on road)
TIME: 4 hours
MAPS: O.S. 1:25 000 Outdoor Leisure: 24-White Peak (east)

This excellent all weather route is mainly formed by cunningly linked pieces of unclassified road. It is a good route for café stops. Also there are villages with historical interest. Eyam especially is noted for its architecture and for its selfless restraint when the Plague swept through the village in the 17th century.

Start in Baslow at the Park Side public carpark SK 258721. Turn left out of the carpark. Go left at the roundabout (signposted 'Bakewell, Buxton, Chatsworth, Rowsley, Haddon'). Then take the second proper road right which is signposted 'Bakewell A619, Buxton A6'. Nearly a mile up this road, on your right, above a stream, you should see a large gate with a sign on it saying 'Unsuitable for Motors'.

Go through this gate and along a well surfaced track. You should be able to see a small stone barn ahead of you with four arched windows. Follow the track through the wood, ignoring a track left uphill, then descend to ford a small stream and then climb gently up a narrower walled path. You will pass through about three gates before coming to the road at Hassop.

Turn right, then just round the corner take the first road left (signposted 'Great Longstone and Rowland') past the opulent entrance to Hassop Hall. Follow it for about three quarters of a mile. It climbs uphill then levels. Take the first road signposted 'Rowland, Only'. Ride up through the village and past Top Farm. The tarmac gives way to a gravel track and there is a welcome 'Unsuitable for Motors' sign. Continuing up this track you should be able to see the curved wall of an underground reservoir above you, to your right.

Shortly after passing this take the walled track left. It is very steep, loosely surfaced and bordered by elder and other trees.

After considerable effort you should reach a metal five-bar gate. Go through it, across a narrow tongue of land that appears to have been mined in the past and straight on uphill through a second large gate. The path becomes single track, more rutted and very difficult to ride. You will soon reach a large quarry track. You are now at High Rake. Watch out for **huge** quarry lorries and even larger quarries. Turn right, following the track downhill for about 400 metres before turning left opposite the entrance to Bleaklow Farm. You cross the rate at the first available point, a section that has been in-filled, near newly planted trees.

Go through the wooden bridlegate beside the larger five-bar and follow the bridleway, a grass track, as it climbs gently and curves left to another gate. Pass through this and descend the walled green lane. At the bottom go through a gate, cross a bridleway and join the gravel track.

You should be on the left of two gravel tracks running side by side. Curve right uphill. When two tracks merge remain on the left-hand track which skirts along the edge of a huge 'sludge lagoon'. On meeting a small road, turn right, right again and almost immediately left down tarmac into Wardlow. At the village of Wardlow a right turn will take you to the busy A623 road at Wardlow Mires. At the A623 turn left signposted 'Stockport and Manchester'. Peter's Stone is on your left. Take the next road right. It is only very small and signposted 'Access Only'. Take care turning off the main road. You are in a dip, hidden from the fast-moving traffic.

Once on the small road you drop into a dip, curve left and climb slightly. Take the right turn towards Stanley House marked with a dead-end sign.

At Stanley House the tarmac disappears and you should turn ninety degrees left on a stony track. This track has limestone walls on either side, twisting and bulging as if ready to collapse any minute. They will probably stay like that for fifty years! These drystone walls, typical of the area, stretch for miles, surrounding fields that are by today's standards very small. The track narrows as it branches left to run parallel with Silly Dale. Follow it to a road junction where you should go straight across towards Grindlow.

Pass through Grindlow on the road. Turn right at the T-junction near Great Hucklow, to follow a signpost saying 'Gliding Club and Bretton'.

It is uphill again, but is rideable! After less than half a mile there is a road left signposted 'Gliding Club and Abney'. A little way past this on the right is a track. Ignore the track but take the narrow path right, just above it. This RUPP along Hucklow Edge is slightly downhill. It is narrow, rutted and often muddy, with bush and scrub either side and a good view to the right. When you meet the road on a very steep corner, turn left uphill. The road you are on soon flattens out and is joined by a road from the left. You will pass Bretton YHA on your left then should turn left just before the Barrel Inn.

This downhill track curves right and offers good views left out towards Bretton Clough. The tarmac is soon replaced by a stony surface. After about half a mile you will come out at a road, again on a corner.

Turn immediately left onto the gravel track marked 'Unsuitable for Motors' and follow it over Broadlow and Sir William Hill, passing a huge aerial. Ride down a straight section to meet the Eyam to Grindleford road. Bear right onto this road towards Eyam.

You will pass the famous Mompesson's Well then should turn right towards Highcliffe (signposted 'Bretton, Abney and Great Hucklow'). Half a mile along this road you will come to Highcliffe Farm. Turn left opposite the farm to follow a steep mud and rock track. This winding unclassified road descends steeply into the village of Eyam.

On reaching the road proper, on a corner, turn right. Ride downhill past the carpark, then go left on the road to Town End, passing Eyam Hall on the way. Several roads converge at Town End, which could be considered the centre of Eyam village. There are a number of shops including a chip shop.

Immediately below (or above) Eyam Tea Rooms turn right. These two tarmac tracks/roads merge. Follow the tarmac road to a farm. Go left down the track beside the farm in roughly a south-easterly direction. Tarmac soon peters out as this pleasant unclassified road descends towards Stoney Middleton. Pass through two gates as necessary. On reaching the main road (A623) at Stoney Middleton turn left and follow it about a mile and a quarter to Calver, passing straight ahead at the traffic lights.

The next road left says 'Calver Mill'. Take this option then curve right to cross the River Derwent. Immediately after the bridge are two left turns, the first to Froggatt and the second, which you want, to Curbar village.

There is now a vicious hill up through Curbar village, to Curbar Gap. It is the point at which the road passes between the dramatic Curbar and Baslow gritstone edges, part of a chain of such edges than runs down the eastern flank of the Peak. At the top of the hill is a carpark on your left. Just before this go right through one of the bridlegates onto Baslow Edge.

Savour the view. You have earned it! Follow the larger left-hand track (bridleway) along Baslow Edge until there is a track turning right. At this point you will be able to see Wellington's Monument (a stone cross) a little further on to your left. You will need to go down the track to the right (however if you wish to, you could ride along the rest of the edge, before returning to this point).

Eventually descend the very rough steep track into Baslow, passing through a gate as necessary. On meeting the main road in Baslow turn left and follow it back to your starting point.

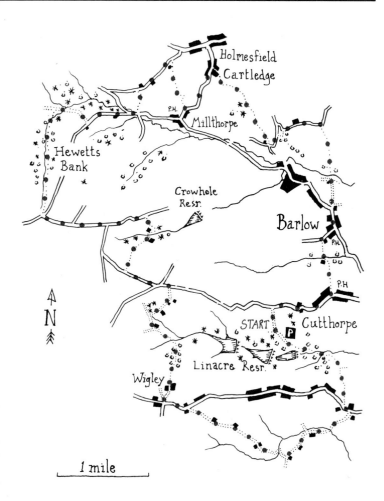

Holmesfield
Cartledge

P.H.
Millthorpe

Hewetts
Bank

Crowhole
Resr.

Barlow

P.H.

P.H

START   Cutthorpe
P

Linacre Resr.

Wigley

N

1 mile

LINACRE

Linacre Reservoir, Ashgate, Riddings, Wigley, Birley, Moorhall, Hewetts Bank, Horsleygate, Cartledge, Barlow, Cutthorpe, Linacre Reservoir Circle.

DISTANCE: 17¹/₂ miles/28km (6mls/10km on road)
TIME: 4¹/₂ hours
MAPS: O.S. 1:25 000: Outdoor Leisure 24-White Peak (east)
Pathfinder 761 Chesterfield and
Stoney Middleton sheet SK 27/37

Linacre Reservoirs, the starting point for this ride, are surrounded by mixed woodland; elm, ash, and oak as well as larch and conifers. There are two nature trail walks of one and two miles. Our cycle route links interesting stretches of bridleway often used by horses. The countryside is undulating and dotted with reservoirs. There are a number of streams to cross. Quite large areas of land are owned by the water authority. In clear weather the hilltops give panoramic views of the surrounding area. Often you can look back on the stretch of route you have just covered.

The tracks, generally not too rocky, tend to be either sand/gravel farm tracks or narrow muddy paths, some doubling as streams. Stretches of this route do get very muddy but we have tried to arrange it so that these are downhill. Even in very wet weather you shouldn't need to walk more than half a mile in all.

Start at Linacre Reservoir main carpark SK 336728. Turn left out of the carpark onto the bridleway towards Ashgate. Downhill, in a south-easterly direction, it is at first a tarmac surface but soon becomes a wide track of mud and stone. Go through or round the large metal gate before crossing Linacre Brook to follow the larger of the tracks as it climbs out of the woods and passes Woodnook Cottage. Ignore the small footpath that veers off left and the track left to the housing estate. Follow the track you are on to a road.

Turn left onto the road but then right after only about 200 metres onto the signposted bridleway. When this hard-packed farm track forks, bear right. A slight descent is followed by a gentle climb. About half a mile will bring you to Broomhall Farm. Continue along the track you are on, ignoring a bridleway right just after the farm. Climb to Westwick Farm then, about 200 metres past this turn right opposite a large bungalow.

This bridleway, at first a metalled drive, descends through a farm and crosses a stream before climbing uphill. It soon becomes rocky (though the next half mile can get very boggy too). Pass through Frith Hall. Depending on the weather there may be a pond across the track with ducks on it! Continue climbing up the track. At the next farm, The Birches, follow the bridleway to curve ninety degrees left.

Beyond Bagthorpe Farm the track levels out, is harder and drier. On meeting the tarmac road opposite the Royal Oak turn left. Take the next right signposted 'Wigley' and marked as a dead-end. Follow tarmac to Wigley Hall Farm ignoring a footpath left. Just left of the farm take the narrow path into the 'bush', following the wooden fingerpost ('Reservoirs'). This narrow indistinct mud path through the vast array of brambles, bushes and shrubs descends parallel to the wall to your left, and further down, to the stream.

On reaching an oak tree where the path forks, drop steeply downhill to the left on an entertaining stretch of path to a stream. Go left, ford one stream, then up the left-hand side of another and between stone gateposts. Cross right, over this second stream to a gate. The gate marks the start of a walled lane. Follow this uphill. It curves left after only 100 metres then eventually joins a tarmac drive.

Ride up this very smooth drive past a large house (Birley Farm). After a short distance turn right opposite a pond (there may also be a ford). Follow this rough track up to the next road junction.

Turn left onto the road then second right after only 250 metres. Descend for half a mile to where a bridleway leaves the road to the right. It is a large metal gate (sign saying 'Grange Lumb Farm') and also has a fingerpost.

Go through the gate and down the hard track, then through the gate just left of the farm. Ride down a muddy track to cross the stream which feeds Crowhole Reservoir.

Climb to a gate and pass through the nearby Grangewood Farm. Continue on a farm track to the road. Go left and follow the road for about three quarters of a mile ignoring one left and one right turn-off.

You should come to a T-junction with a bridlegate and track opposite. This is the top of Hewetts Bank. Go straight across the road through the small gate to join this track. After only about 100 metres take the right-hand fork. You now have got about a mile of straight descent to come, but it is a well-used track that can get quite churned up in wet weather. Descend until you cross the stream, then at the next bridlegate turn right onto a larger track.

This track drops down before a steep climb (you will need a good run up!) mainly on tarmac. Near the top a farm drive joins from the right. Continue up to meet the road. Turn left and descend steeply to a road T-junction. Go right then after crossing a stream immediately left, on a bridleway up into the woods.

This path, heavily lined with oak and holly, is narrow and steep but short and pleasant too. Turn right at the road. Pass some very fine houses in Horsleygate then after roughly half a mile, beside the 'Little Orchard' house, a metal fingerpost points right. This says 'Bridleway to Millthorpe $1/2$ mile'. It is all downhill but the surface varies, some of it being muddy.

Ford at Hewetts Bank

At the second small gate, you have to cross a stream before meeting the Millthorpe road. Turn left uphill (unless you first want to visit the pub in Millthorpe).

Assuming you turn left (or come back to this point after dinner), climb steeply about half a mile up the road to Cartledge Hall where a fingerpost right says 'Footpath and Bridleway to Brindwoodgate for Barlow'. Take this bridleway right, follow the track past the farm and descend to a point where you meet a large wooden five-bar gate and a field in front of you.

Here you need to curve right to follow the narrower re-surfaced path. It winds downhill between trees and hedges to a small gate. Soon you meet a road. Turn left, then left again on a very sharp corner. Unfortunately it is uphill!

After about 200 metres turn right on the track marked 'Unsuitable for Motors'. Follow this uphill (ignore a footpath right) until a road where you should turn right. After about half a mile of descent, on a sharp left- hand corner, turn right onto a bridleway. It soon becomes muddy single track, widens out then is single track again. You will have to negotiate two gates. When the path forks take the right-hand option. Cross Dunston Brook at the bottom of the woods before climbing steeply up the tarmac road to Elm Tree Farm.

On meeting the B6051 turn left into Barlow. Turn right in front of the Peacock Hotel and climb up the road for about 400 metres before taking the bridleway left (just past national speed restriction signs). This muddy overgrown narrow path descends to ford Sud Brook. Then climb a steep mud track and go left on tarmac until you reach a proper T-junction at Cutthorpe. Turn right here and follow the road slightly uphill for less than half a mile, passing a pub and school.

Take the first proper road left which is the entrance to Linacre Reservoir carpark where you started your ride!

*2002 Carry straight on after crossing Linacre Brook

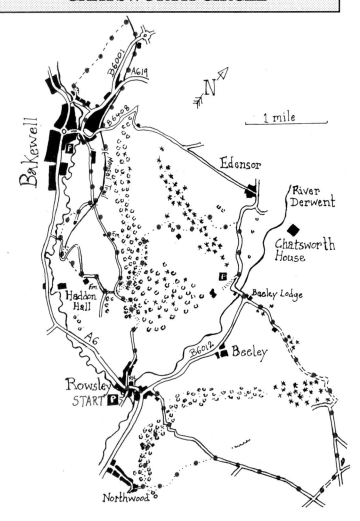

CHATSWORTH

Rowsley, Bouns Corner, Bakewell, Monsal Trail, Manners Wood, New Piece Wood, Chatsworth, Beeley Moor, Northwood Carr, Copy Wood, Rowsley Circle.

DISTANCE: 19 miles/30$^{1}/_{2}$km (5mls/8km on road)
TIME: 3$^{1}/_{2}$ hours
MAPS: O.S. 1:25 000 Outdoor Leisure: 24-White Peak (east)

This route passes through the grounds of two famous houses (Chatsworth House and Haddon Hall). There are ample opportunities for refreshments especially in Bakewell and Rowsley. The route can easily be shortened or lengthened as you please. Mostly the landscape is rolling parkland, limestone farmland, gritstone moors or deciduous woodland with plenty of hills. You will see grouse, pheasants, sheep and perhaps deer, as well as wild flowers and fine views of Derbyshire. There are gravel, grass and soil tracks, with some ex-railway line too. Some stretches of the route can be soggy in wet weather.

Start in Rowsley behind Cauldwell Mill, (Flour Milling Museum) at the free carpark, SK 256657. Turn left out of the carpark and after 100 metres you will meet the A6. Opposite should be the Peacock Hotel. Cross the A6 and go up the road just left of the hotel marked as a dead-end. After 600 metres uphill on tarmac, this road becomes a bridleway; a mud and stone track which climbs a further 400 metres into woodland.

Just as you enter the wood proper (Bouns Corner) there are two metal gates and several converging paths. Continue along the lowest of the tracks, left. Soon there is a clearing and a track forking to the right. Ride straight on downhill.

On reaching a metal gate with a fine vista (SK 244669) there are three options; left, right or straight on. Turn left, slightly uphill. The track flattens out. As you curve gently to the right ignore the track branching off to your left. It is soon downhill and you will pass a farm entrance on your left. The track itself soon curves right into a field but you should go straight on, following the narrow overgrown waymarked path. To your left is Bowling Green Farm. Yes it has got one! Peer over the wall and you'll see it. Presumably the inhabitants of the 14th century Haddon Hall would saunter up for a genteel game after high tea.

Go through a small gate then hug the bottom fence (metal) for three fields. You are now in the park/grounds of Haddon Hall (home of the Duke of Rutland). The hall is just below you, to your left, but is hidden from view.

When you meet a tarmac track turn left. It drops steeply with sharp bends. Ignore the small fork right. Continue down towards the River Wye but look for the first bridleway right which is a waymarked wooden gate beside a

larger metal gate. Go through the small gate onto the field and aim for the old ash tree. Follow the sheep paths which contour round the field just above the trees. On reaching a fence, stay this side of it but turn right, up the field. At the top of the field go through the small wooden gate and turn left onto the cinder/gravel track.

In May a dense blanket of bluebells usually covers the bank to your right. The track brings you out just by the old railway viaduct (Coombs Viaduct). Turn left and follow the minor road into Bakewell.

You will come out at the junction between the B6408 and the A619 near the river. A stone pinnacle sits in the centre of the road. Turn right up the A road and after about 400 metres go left along Holme Lane. On your left you will soon see a packhorse bridge over the river. Go right opposite this on a bridleway (stone track) which climbs steeply through an old quarry. Go through the gate and onto fields, passing another old quarry and cow pond before a second gate leads into a stretch of walled lane. Follow this bridleway down over bumpy fields, alongside the wall until you meet the old railway (Monsal Trail).

Turn right and follow the railway for over two miles until you meet a gate across the track and a sign just in front of it which says 'End of Trail'.

Leave the trail here. Drop down onto a well-surfaced track/road. Turn left, pass under the now familiar viaduct and ride uphill past Coombs Farm. You will climb steadily uphill to reach the point you were at earlier in the ride (SK 244669). This time take the steepest uphill path; the mud one, left into the woods. At the next track T-junction turn left uphill then after a short distance turn right to climb even more steeply.

Luckily this bridleway soon levels before curving right through a stone gateway. You curve immediately left. Continue through the thinned work area until a sharp right turn, through a gap in the wall, brings you to a stile and double gate. Descend across the fields bearing slightly left. Aim for roughly halfway along the plantation below. The bridleway is marked by wooden posts.

You should join a mud track and come to a gate. Go through the gap in the plantation via this large gate then turn right to follow the bottom wall. You soon come to another gate where a track bears left. Head left up this track/bridleway, and go through New Piece Wood.

As you come out of the wood you should get a good view of Chatsworth House (home of the Duke of Devonshire with famous gardens designed by Joseph Paxton) below. Ride downhill on grass to the first waymarking post. Fork right here just above the young trees. Follow the wide, flat grass track parallel to the top wall before dropping diagonally right over the grass to join the road at Lindup Low. Turn right down the road, ride over the humpback bridge then turn immediately left just above Beeley Lodge.

Head up the steep unclassified road towards the moors. There is now a steady climb of a good mile and a half. Tarmac soon gives way to a rough but dry stony farm track. On meeting the road at the top turn left. Climb up the road and ignore the road which forks left. Take the first right turn which is roughly a mile from where you left Beeley Plantation.

It is a rough gravelly track opposite a road turning left (in season there might be an ice cream van here at weekends). Ride along the rough potholed track until you meet the road again. Turn right and go downhill. There is a road off left which should be ignored and then a slight rise. The road flattens out. Just before a right-hand corner and the brow of the hill turn left off the road through double wooden gates.

The obvious path among the sheep descends over the moor above Fallinge Edge. There are fine surrounding views. A wooded section with muddy patches follows. As the path curves right you'll see a stream to your left. The path forks. Take the higher path, right, which is narrow, reasonably flat and contours through Northwood Carr along the side of the hill for about half a mile to a small bridlegate.

After this gate go down the track to your left for only twenty metres to a junction of paths. You need to go through two large gates so that you cross the track in front of you and continue straight on into Copy Woods. A mud path with some bumps takes you along to a road. Go left, very steeply downhill into Rowsley.

Turn left at the bottom and then turn right onto the A6. Pass over the river before turning left to finish back at Cauldwell Mill carpark.

On the Middleton-by-Youlgreave route

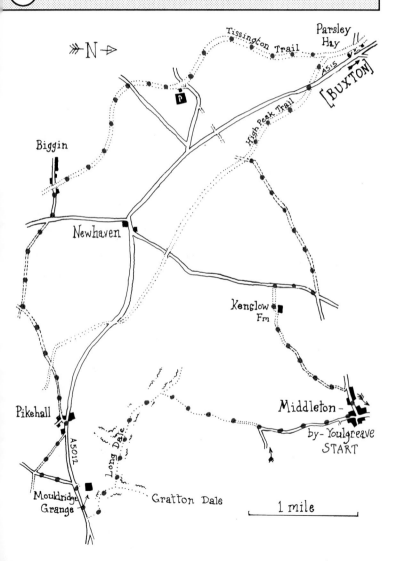

≫N⇥

Tissington Trail

Parsley Hay

A515

BUXTON

P

High Peak Trail

Biggin

Newhaven

Kenslow Fm

Pikehall

A5012

Long Dale

Middleton-
by-Youlgreave
START

Mouldridge
Grange

Gratton Dale

1 mile

MIDDLETON-BY-YOULGREAVE

Long Dale, Pikehall, Biggin,Tissington Trail, Parsley Hay, High Peak Trail, Middleton-by-Youlgreave Circle.

DISTANCE: 15 miles/24km (3mls/5km on road)
TIME: 3 hours
MAPS: O.S. 1:25 000 Outdoor Leisure: 24-White Peak (east & west)

This route is on hilly limestone farmland mainly in open countryside, with largely gravel surfaces or soil tracks with some grass. It also includes small sections of both the High Peak and Tissington trails; flat disused railway lines, ideal for, and well used by, both walkers and cyclists. There are short muddy stretches in wet weather but generally surfaces are good (nothing too rough). This route could be ridden on a touring bike.

Start in Middleton-by-Youlgreave SK 195632.

If you want the option, you can extend this ride by linking it to the Darley Bridge Circle which would add another 18mls/29km but bring you back to this point.

For the standard Middleton-by-Youlgreave route, from Middleton take the road south towards Dale End and Elton. Roughly three quarters of a mile on, after a downhill stretch, the road climbs gently. There is a sharp left-hand corner before the road reaches Smerrill Grange Farm. On this corner, uphill to the right, are two tracks, the first an old walled path lined with trees and vegetation, the second, a wide gravel track up the fields. Take the first track.

This joins the gravel path and continues to climb quite steeply. After a gate it curves gently right. Follow the obvious track until another gate brings you onto a large squarish field with lumps of limestone in its upper right-hand corner. These are the remains of an ancient burial mound. Follow the left-hand wall of this field and the next. After a gate you will come onto the side of Long Dale.

Join the path which traverses left along the top of the dale before descending diagonally into it. Long Dale is a small steep-sided grassy dale which is usually quiet. You will soon come to two gates. Go through the small wooden gate left rather than the large metal five-bar straight on. Follow Long Dale until it meets the head of Gratton Dale.

At this point go through the gate and turn right. Follow the path as it climbs up and then winds round the hill to the left, passing through another gateway. Head right across to the limestone wall then follow it to the A5012.

Turn right onto the road then take the first left opposite Mouldridge Grange (signposted 'Parwich'). About half a mile up this road, just before a right-hand bend, turn right onto the unclassified road. Ride down this walled track to Holly Bush Farm and the main road. Turn left. After 100 metres go left onto a smaller road.

You are now in Pikehall and should turn right onto the unclassified road which runs just under Cottage Farm. This gravel track climbs uphill, becoming grassy and rutted further up. After less than half a mile you should cross the High Peak Trail. Another half mile should bring you to a T-junction. Turn right. A mile-long downhill stretch will take you to the A515 (Ashbourne to Buxton road).

Go right then immediately left on a road signposted 'Biggin'. You will soon see a bridge crossing the road. On the near side of the bridge, to the right, a small path leads onto the Tissington Trail. Turn right to follow it north. The smooth cinder surface should prove pleasant riding.

After roughly three miles the High Peak Trail will intercept your route at an acute angle from the right. Eight hundred metres on, is Parsley Hay picnic site and cycle-hire centre. If it is open you can buy sweets and drinks here. Turn around and ride back in the opposite direction, this time taking the left fork to head down the High Peak Trail.

After about three quarters of a mile you have to pass through two gates and cross a track which cuts across the trail. When you come to the next similar track and single gate leave the trail by turning left onto the unclassified road. This undulating hard-packed track will take you about a mile and a half down to a tarmac road. At this road junction turn right towards Newhaven.

Take the first track left off the road after about half a mile. It passes below Kenslow Farm and skirts just right of a wall for about three fields. Where the track forks by a cow pond (the right downhill appearing to go into a small dale) choose the track left and uphill. The track becomes a tarmac road which descends steeply. Be ready for two severe left-hand bends especially the second. You will come out on a steep road above Middleton Hall. Turn right here and drop into Middleton-by-Youlgreave to finish.

MIDDLETON-BY-YOULGREAVE CIRCLE/DARLEY BRIDGE CIRCLE LINK
The Middleton-by-Youlgreave and Darley Bridge Circles overlap. So if you want to make a much longer ride you can combine both to make a large figure of eight shaped route. See the notes in the route descriptions. On each sketch map the point at which the other route overlaps is shown by small feathered arrows.

Salters' Lane, Darley Bridge Circle

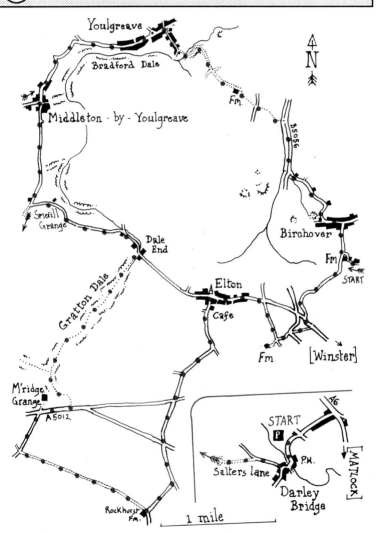

Youlgreave

Bradford Dale

N

Middleton - by - Youlgreave

Fm

B5056

Snitsill Grange

Dale End

Birchover

Fm

START

Gratton Dale

Elton

Cafe

Fm

[Winster]

M'ridge Grange

A5012

Rockhurst Fm.

START
P

Salters Lane

P.H.

Darley Bridge

A6

[MATLOCK]

1 mile

DARLEY BRIDGE

Salters Lane, Upper Town, Elton, Mouldridge Grange, Gratton Dale,
Middleton-by-Youlgreave, Youlgreave, Birchover, Darley Bridge Circle.

DISTANCE: 18 miles/29km (10mls/16km on road)
TIME: 3 hours
MAPS: O.S. 1:25 000 Outdoor Leisure: 24-White Peak (east)

**This is a fine route using bridleways, an old salters' lane and stretches
of unclassified road (probably part of old packhorse routes). The
landscape is a mixture of hilly limestone farmland and woodland, with
small quiet villages linked by twisting roads. There are gravel and
soil tracks, some of them rocky, with fields and dales as well. Some
stretches can be muddy in wet weather.**

Start at Darley Bridge picnic site and carpark SK 270623. Turn right out
of the carpark onto the road. Pass the Square and Compass pub and cross
the river. Take the first road right, signposted 'Stanton Lees', which forks
after 400 metres. Take the left fork, so that as you pass the buildings and
large chimneys of Enthoven's Lead Smelting Works they are all on your
right.

On entering the edge of Clough Woods the track forks. The left fork
descends to Millclose Mine, once Derbyshire's largest and most prolific
lead mine. You want to take the right fork which soon splits again. The
lower flatter track goes through a wooden gate marked Sabine Hay; the
other track, which you want, climbs steeply into the woods.

This is an old salters' lane passing through very pleasant mixed woodland
(with plenty of wild flowers) to Upper Town. It is a loose-surfaced rocky
track of about a mile in length which at first climbs quite steeply but then
levels out and is easily rideable. Near the top of this track you go through
the yard of Uppertown Farm before meeting a road at a T-junction, with
some restored 'stocks' opposite.

Turn left here steeply down the road. Take care since there are blind
corners and the road is wide enough for only a car or a bike, not both! It
flattens out, then climbs slightly and meets the road to Winster. Turn left
onto the road and then almost immediately right onto a RUPP beside Winster
Burial Ground. This RUPP is both rocky and narrow, but short and
interesting.

When you meet the B5056 cross with care. **Please walk up the track
signposted Westhills Farm, since the next 200 metres is a footpath!**
On joining another track with a sign saying 'Limestone Way' you can now
re-mount. Turn right and follow it until you meet a road. Turn left onto the
road which will take you to Elton.

On reaching Elton Church (to your right), go left up the road opposite, beside the Duke of York pub. Elton café, which boasts a fine selection of enamel signs and pretty good cakes, should be on your left. On Sundays it is a favourite haunt of the 'roadie' club cyclists and tourers too so there is good company. Ride up the road and as it curves right ignore the road off left (signposted 'Picnic Site'). You will soon reach a high point with good views. The road levels out then goes downhill.

Go straight across the next two roads you meet. You now have to climb slightly. Again the road curves right and there is a left turn (to Aldwark) you should ignore. Further on where the road veers sharply left, turn right onto an unclassified road below Rockhurst Farm. We have known the top stretch of this track to be a foot deep in silage! Follow this stony/gravel track downhill for about a good mile until you come out on a small road.

Turn right and on meeting the A5012 go right again. Mouldridge Grange should be on your left. After 450 metres, on your left is a gate and a post marked 'Bridleway'. Turn left here onto the field and follow the limestone wall straight on, then round to the left. Next the bridleway cuts diagonally right across the grass field down to an indistinct track through a gateway. This bumpy path curves right and down to two gates where Long Dale, (to your left) and Gratton Dale (straight on) meet.

Go through the small gate into the steep-sided rocky Gratton Dale and follow the path slightly downhill. This is a very bumpy rocky section which can be muddy and is not the place to ride your normal touring iron. Take care on any type of bike. When you come to the road at the bottom you will probably be glad you have. You are at Dale End. Turn left. Soon the road forks and you should go left up a steep but short climb. The road then descends.

If you want to, before finishing this ride you can extend it from here by doing the Middleton-by-Youlgreave Circle as well which would add another 15mls/24km but bring you back to this point.

Follow this road to Middleton-by-Youlgreave, a pleasant small village but without a shop or pub. In mid to late May decorative wall dressings can be seen here. Pass through the village (unless you'd like a pleasant walk down Bradford Dale) and when you meet a larger road turn right.

Ride down the road into Youlgreave. You will pass the Farmyard (Free House) Inn and then a large circular stone monument (conduit/reservoir head). Turn next right, with care, on the small road just in front of the imposing stone church and drop steeply.

Ignore the fork right signposted 'Unsuitable For Motors'. After 150 metres, just as the road curves right you should be able to see a small limestone crag, and the river below you. On your left is 'Braemor House'. Turn left just above the house down the narrow bridleway. It is a steep gravel path with a humpback bridge and ford at the bottom. Cross the river and turn left on the tarmac track.

A short way on, you should follow the road as it curves right, uphill away from the river. The bridleway continues uphill. Ignore the track which crosses yours and pass Lower Greenfields Farm on your right. The tarmac deteriorates and you will come to another larger farm on your right. Pass through the small gate just left of the larger five-bar. Ride straight on across the field, almost following the right-hand wall. You should come to a gate beside a large ash tree. Again go straight across the next field to join a back road (to Elton).

Cross the road, and pass through the gate opposite. Ride straight across the field to a medium sized bridlegate. As you begin to descend more steeply curve right, passing under the small wooded area before joining the path that leads to a gate and small bridge across a stream. Ride diagonally right to join the road and turn right.

A short way up this road take the first road left up to Birchover. It enters the village by the Druid Inn. From here you have two options:

(A) Turn right in Birchover just above the Methodist chapel, onto the small road to Upper Town, then go down the salters' lane you came up at the start of the ride, back to Darley Bridge.

(B) Follow the road up out of Birchover. Turn first right in front of Stanton Park Quarry (gritstone), ride down to Stanton Lees and then turn right again to Darley Bridge, all on the road. Take care as these roads are very steep and winding with blind corners.

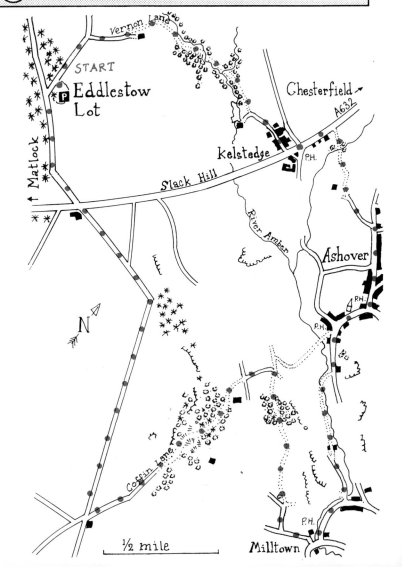

Vernon Lane

START
Eddlestow
Lot

Chesterfield →

A632

↑ Matlock

Slack Hill

Kelstedge

P.H.

River Amber

Ashover

P.H.

P.H.

N

Coffin Lane

P.H.

½ mile

Milltown

ASHOVER

Eddlestow Lot, Vernon Lane, Kelstedge, Ashover, Abrahams Lane, Milltown, Coffin Lane, Eddlestow Lot, Circle.

DISTANCE: 7¹/₂ miles/12km (3mls/5km on road)
TIME: 1¹/₂ hours
MAPS: O.S. 1:25 000 Pathfinder
               778 Bakewell and Matlock sheet SK 26/36

This map covers the whole route, but most is also on the O.S. 1:25 000 Outdoor Leisure 24, White Peak map. Sections that are not, should be easy to follow using the route description and sketch map.

This is a short ride but one well worth doing. It passes through some very pleasant deciduous woodland with a good range of wild flowers and includes several stream crossings. A lot of the paths are quite narrow and sometimes overgrown. The rock/mud/sand surfaces can become heavy going when wet.

Start SK 324632 at Eddlestow Lot carpark/picnic site, Wirestone Quarry (disused). Turn right out of the carpark and ride down the road for about 300 metres. Take the first gravel track right. This is Vernon Lane. A short way down this track you'll come to a farm gateway with steel gates and a small millstone set into the wall. **Go down the waymarked path just left of the gates.** Narrow with a rocky/sandy surface and steeply downhill, this path is rideable but remember horses and walkers use it too! Follow this path down through pleasant mixed woodland.

It flattens out, then comes to a ford beside a small stone bridge. Cross the stream as you see fit and follow the wider path straight on (ignore the small path left) to another ford and bridge. Again go straight on following the main path out of the woods along tarmac to meet the A632 at Kelstedge.

Turn left up the A632. Pass the Kelstedge Inn and a turn off to Ashover, both on your right, then just beyond Bungalow Farm and national speed restriction road signs turn right down the green lane towards Marsh Green. Again it is quite a bumpy rutted path that can be muddy. Drop downhill, ride through a small ford and along the main track until you come out at a road (where a footpath goes right). Go left and up to a T-junction. Here take the road right, into Ashover.

Ride past Ashover Post Office then curve right passing the Crispin Inn and the church on your right. As you come to the next T-junction you should face the Red Lion Inn. Turn left here onto Hockley Lane. Ignore the first bridleway almost immediately right. Ride down the road for about 300 metres then take the bridleway (Abrahams Lane) which leaves the road by going right opposite two small houses. It is only narrow so don't miss it! Follow Abrahams Lane down to, and then parallel with, the stream. The path

crosses the stream (River Amber) on a fine stone slab bridge then follows the other bank until a farm and barn clad with corrugated iron.

Go through the farm. Turn left when you meet a road, roll gently downhill curving to the right and you should come out on a tarmac road at a large quarry entrance. Cross a bridge over the stream, then turn immediately right. Follow this road to the Miners Arms pub. Turn right here. When the road forks, veer right slightly uphill.

After 200 metres the road curves sharply left and there is a quarry entrance to your right. On this corner leave the road to follow an overgrown path (unclassified road) directly ahead of you. You will climb slightly into the woods on a narrow mud and stone path. Follow it up and down for roughly half a mile to a clearing where a wider gravel track crosses yours. Ashover should be visible down to your right and the small path in front of you is edged with stone slabs on end. Turn left onto the larger track here and follow it for 200 metres to another large gravel track.

To the left is Overton Hall. Continue along the bridleway you are on by crossing straight over the large track. Ride up the 'Coffin Lane' paved with stone slabs into the woods. After passing through the woods colonised by huge rhododendrons you will come out onto old mine spoil heaps below the gritstone Cocking Tor. Follow the same line as the path took through the woods. Ride over the spoil heaps gaining not losing height, traversing round the hill to join a muddy track which climbs more steeply towards Ravensnest.

This becomes tarmac and climbs to Red House Farm where you come to a road junction. From here on is all road. Turn right and follow the very straight road for about a mile. The road bends sharp left before joining the A632 at the top of Slack Hill. Turn left then immediately right signposted 'Beeley, Darley Dale'. The next right-hand turn leads back to your starting point.

Coffin Lane

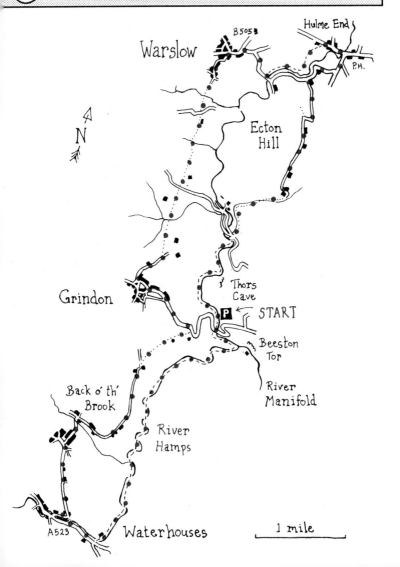

Hulme End

B505

Warslow

P.H.

Ecton
Hill

N

Thors
Cave

Grindon

P ← START

Beeston
Tor

Back o' th'
Brook

River
Manifold

River
Hamps

Waterhouses

A523

1 mile

MANIFOLD

Weag's Bridge, Manifold Valley Light Railway (Manifold Way), Waterhouses, Waterfall, Grindon, Warslow, Hulme End, Back of Ecton, Light Railway, Weag's Bridge Circle.

DISTANCE: 18miles/29km (5mls/8km on road)
TIME: 5 hours
MAPS: O.S. 1:25 000 Outdoor Leisure 24 - White Peak (west)

Straddling the Derbyshire/Staffordshire border, through deep valleys and across limestone upland, this route includes dramatic views and striking geological features. The valley of the River Manifold and the track of the old light railway (closed 1934) form part of the route. The river vanishes down swallow holes, there are caves with evidence of early man, and fine rock outcrops. The wooded valley twists and turns between steep and sometimes conical hills.

Once on the uplands it's high, open sheep country with limestone walls and the occasional ash or hawthorn. Finishing back in the Manifold Valley the route passes within quarter of a mile of Wettonmill with its mediaeval farm, café and campsite.

This area did have a good network of bridleways and RUPPs so that a range of off-road rides was possible. However, quite a few were downgraded to footpaths. This route therefore includes a fair amount of tarmac riding. It is mostly traffic free however, and the route as a whole is still a good taster to a splendid area.

Start in the carpark lay-by near Weag's Bridge SK 100542. Standing with your back to the river turn left out of the lay-by, cross the small road (but not the river), and go through the small gate onto the right of the two tarmac tracks in front of you. This is the Manifold Way, which used to be a light railway. At first you will ride alongside the River Manifold but then you curve right (the large crag above you to the left is Beeston Tor) and wind along, crossing back and forth over the River Hamps. After following this flat track for about two and a half miles you will meet the A523 at Waterhouses.

At the A523 cross the fast road with care and turn right onto a cycle track. Cycle along for nearly half a mile before taking the first right turn opposite the Post Office. Cross the river on a humpback bridge and follow this road. You will curve right then begin to climb uphill.

Roughly three quarters of a mile should bring you to a junction. Continue straight on but take the next right turn after only 100 metres. This road sweeps downhill and through a ford to Back o' th' Brook. After the ford curve right up the road with a dead-end sign. It traverses up and round the hill for a good half mile before reaching a white wooden gate saying 'Private, No Parking'.

Go through this and up the track to the farm, where two more gates take you through the yard. Watch out for a goose. Next go through the metal five-bar gate in front of you before dropping down the field on the track, slightly to the left. You should aim to go through the metal gate into the L-shaped field with the cow pond in it. Follow the grass track uphill to the right where there is a gateway at the highest point of the field. From the gateway go straight ahead so you cut off the right-hand corner of the field but rejoin the right-hand wall by hawthorn trees.

Now follow this right-hand edge, through one bridlegate, across another field and then through a second gate. Keep following this edge for the next field too, until you reach a slightly larger gate in the corner.

Go through the gate then drop diagonally down the grass field aiming just left of the stone barn. As you approach the corner of the field wall attached to the barn, curve right round it through a gate. Drop down the bank to the bridlegate and up the steep field following the right-hand wall. Keep close to the right hand wall. After two gateways you should meet a very steep road.

If you want to cut the ride short here, turn right down the road. It is less than quarter of a mile to your starting point. To continue the ride turn left steeply uphill to Grindon. On the road into the village take the first fork right, to pass a row of terraced houses.

At the church the road curves sharp left. Turn right immediately above the play area, down the road with the dead-end sign. The road dips, down then up, then descends again for 300 or 400 metres. Where the tarmac becomes a stone track, at a large field before the farm buildings, look for a bridlegate and stile on your left.

From here to Warslow is a stretch over grass fields which involves losing and gaining height several times. There are muddy patches and some walking will be needed.

Go through the gate, diagonally across the field, through an open gateway and down the next field to a line of ash and hawthorn. After going through a small gate ride down the left-hand edge of the field to another gate. After this is a damp, rocky path, where I fell off (beware!), down to cross the stream via a small bridge.

Go through the bridlegate, over a very boggy patch (small bridge) then left steeply uphill following the left-hand edge of the field. Continue in this manner over the next three fields negotiating gates as necessary. At the road go straight across through the gate, and down two fields to a farm track. Cross this too, go through the large metal five-bar gate and down two fields with gates, to a long narrow field. Cross diagonally over this, and the next field to cross a stream, go through a small gate and start climbing. Follow the right-hand hedge to the gate. Go straight across the next field to a gate and then follow a stretch of gravelly track to a road.

Thor's Cave

Cross the road and go through the bridlegate opposite into a steep rocky tree-lined walled lane. Some parts may be very difficult to pass.

At the bottom ford the stream (wet feet?), then walk uphill to the bridlegate in the right-hand corner. Another walled stretch and gate bring you to a gravel track in front of houses. Curve right until you meet tarmac then bear left up the road into Warslow.

On meeting the B5053 turn right. Ignore the road off left unless you want to visit the Greyhound pub (welcoming, with home cooked food) but take the next turn right, signposted 'Ecton and Manifold Valley'. Go first right again, down a fine hill, cross the River Manifold and then turn left onto the old light railway.

Follow this to the B5054 at Hulme End. Turn right, then next right signposted 'Wetton and Alstonfield'. Take the next right again, then the first left signposted 'Back of Ecton, No Through Road'. After roughly a mile, at Back of Ecton you should come to a hairpin corner (steeply uphill) where a road forks off left. Take this left downhill, past Lees Farm, through a gate to Manor House. Go through the large wooden gate beside a stream, and follow the stream all the way down the valley. At the bottom cross the road, then the river, back onto the light railway track. Follow this for about a mile due south back to your starting point.

Chevin, Derby North

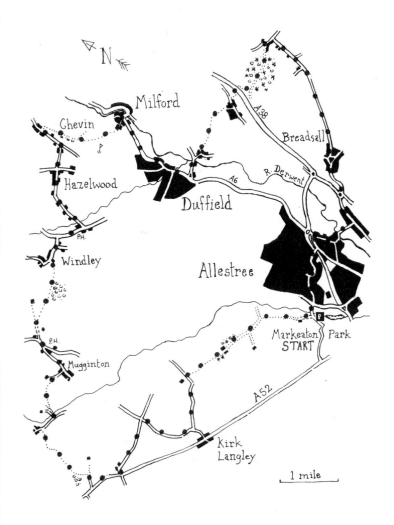

N

Milford

Chevin

Breadsall

A38

R. Derwent

Hazelwood

A6

Duffield

P.H.

Windley

Allestree

P.H.

Muggington

Markeaton Park
START

A52

Kirk Langley

1 mile

DERBY NORTH

Markeaton, Mercaston, Muggington, Windley, Hazelwood, Chevin, Milford, Duffield, Brackely Gate, Breadsall, Markeaton Circle.

DISTANCE:	25 miles/40km (15mls/24km on road)
TIME:	5 hours
MAPS:	O.S. 1:25 000 Pathfinders:
	832 - Derby & Etwall sheet SK 23/33
	811 - Belper sheet SK 24/34

Derby North Circle is an attempt to link up some of the nicer sections of off-road cycling north of Derby. Doing this does involve a fair amount of road work. However the roads used are generally quiet country lanes. Keep an eye out for hedge cuttings and do not forget to take your spare inner tube and puncture repair kit.

Start at the Mundy Play Centre carpark, north of Markeaton Park SK 332380. Heading north out of the carpark turn right then immediately left onto a lane/track. Pass over a cattle grid and past the new houses and buildings of Markeaton Stones. Follow this obvious track for roughly half a mile until a T-junction with a tarmac road. Turn left uphill. Choose the right fork to Upper Vicarwood Farm. Here you need to pass through a large white gate to continue along the bridleway just below the brick stables. Follow the track round the field's edge to a road.

Turn left onto Lodge Lane. After about three quarters of a mile go right towards Mercaston. Ride along Flagshaw Lane for roughly a mile to a crossroads. Take a left turn and cycle to the Ashbourne road (A52T). Turn right towards Brailsford. You need the next right after roughly half a mile and just before a 'Reduce Speed Now' sign. Don't miss it.

Ride along this track until, just before a cattlegrid, there is a left turn. Take this and leave the tarmac behind. This takes you along Woods Lane, a muddy rutted track, which after a good mile rejoins tarmac just outside Mercaston. Turn right onto the road. After 500 metres go left on the track signposted 'Bridleway to Muggington'.

After only 200 metres leave the large gravel track by turning right (following the waymarking arrows). Ride very briefly along a shallow stream to a good path which leads to a bridlegate. From here do not go straight on but ride uphill following the left-hand edge of the next two fields. Descend to a gate. Turn right onto Hunger Lane which climbs to Mugginton.

Take a left turn. Ride half a mile to a road junction (rear of The Cock Inn). Go left but after only 200 metres, turn right. Ride down this track/road. You should soon pass a waste disposal site. Continue along the track passing through three large metal gates (which may be waymarked by blue arrows).

You will come to two more large metal gates, this time side by side. Go through the waymarked left-hand gate and follow the right-hand edge of the field to a bridlegate. Go through this then ride across to and through another gate. Head up to the top of the hill riding parallel to the edge of the woods. Ride down the track (which also follows the wood's edge).

When you meet two five-bar gates do not go straight on but take the right-hand gate (marked A. Valley Routeway No. 2) to cross a field diagonally on a rough track. Continue down this track passing through a large gate/gateway until (where the track bends sharp left) you reach a small bridlegate. Go through the bridlegate then bear left keeping the farm buildings (Chapel Farm) to your right (contrary to the O.S. map which shows the bridleway passing below the farm). A gate takes you out onto the road opposite Windley Baptist Chapel.

From here turn right to follow Windley Lane nearly half a mile to the Wirksworth road. Turn right here. Take the next left onto Nether Lane which climbs to Hazelwood. After just over a mile, at Hazelwood crossroads, go straight on. Take the next left towards Farnah Green.

As you ride downhill, after 500 metres, you should see the Bluebell Inn on your left. Take the signposted bridleroad right just after the Bluebell. This is North Lane, a fine sandy track which takes you south over the top of the Chevin on the line of a pre-historic ridgeway. Watch out for low-flying golf balls from the adjacent golf course!

Descend into Milford. At the bottom, by the Strutt Arms, turn right onto the A6 and follow it for about a mile into Duffield. Go past the shops in Duffield then take the first proper road left (Makeney Road). You will cross the River Derwent on Duffield Bridge, then should turn immediately right past the Bridge Inn. Continue up this road a short way (about 300m) to Eaton Bank. Here, just before the road levels, take the signposted bridleway, back left. At the end of the lane some steps lead up to the right behind a white garage. You will have to get off and shoulder your bike here but should soon be able to re-mount. Ride across to a bridlegate.

Go through this gate then follow the muddy path/bridleway, sticking to the right-hand edge of the fields (and passing through a number of gates as you go) for roughly half a mile. Remember to shut all the gates behind you! You will come to a bridlegate that leads into Eaton Park Woods. Follow the muddy path downhill through this pleasant woodland to come out on Alfreton Road

Turn left and pass the Bell and Harp. There is a bridleroad sign just before the national speed limit sign. Turn right down Toad Lane. Go over a level crossing, over Bottle Brook, straight across Derby Road and under the A38 to a gate. At this point ride left up the field's edge. Go through a gate and turn left onto the lane. Ride steadily uphill on this good sandy track for about a mile through woodland (Horsley Carr). Ignore tracks off to the left and right. You should come out at Brackely Gate.

Turn right, then right again along Quarry Road which leads straight along the line of Ryknild street to Breadsall. This becomes Moor Road as you enter the village of Breadsall. Pass the stone church (with spire) on your left then turn right. Continue until you meet a T-junction. Turn right on Croft Lane signposted 'Derby'.

From here on, back through Derby, you have to cross some very busy, large roads so take extra care. Follow Croft Lane to a large roundabout. Go straight across following the signs to 'Alfreton Road Industrial Estate'. After roughly half a mile take the first right turn, Haslams Lane, between Rolls Royce Composites and Delta Crompton Cables. This leads to Darley Abbey Industrial Estate. Go through the estate, crossing the River Derwent via a Toll Bridge. Cars are sometimes charged £1 at this Toll Bridge!

Cycle up Old Lane to a T-junction where you should turn right onto Church Lane. Continue uphill until you meet Duffield Road (A6). Go left, then after only 400 metres, right up Ferrers Way. Follow this for about half a mile until you meet a T-junction with Birchover Way where you should turn left.

Ride downhill to a road junction. Turn left onto Kedleston Road then immediately right down Markeaton Lane. A short way along this lane on your left is Mundy Play Centre where you started your ride.

*2002 The companies have changed on Haslams Lane and the reduce speed sign on the A52 has gone.

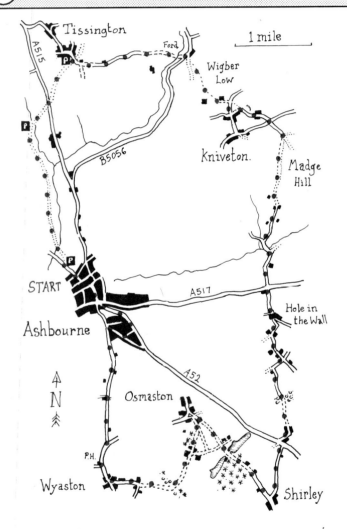

1 mile

Tissington

Ford

Wigber
Low

A515

B5056

Kniveton.

Madge
Hill

P

START

A517

Hole in
the Wall

Ashbourne

A52

Osmaston

N

P.H.

Wyaston

Shirley

ASHBOURNE

Ashbourne, Tissington Trail, Tissington, Tissington Ford, Kniveton, Madge Hill, Moorend, Osmaston Park, Wyaston, Ashbourne Circle.

DISTANCE: 19 miles/30.5km (10mls/16km on road)
TIME: 4¹/₂ hours
MAPS: O.S. 1:25 000 Outdoor Leisure: 24-White Peak (east)
Pathfinders: 811-Belper sheet SK 24/34,
810-Ashbourne and the Churnet Valley sheet SK 04/14

This route has mixed terrain and surfaces including a fair amount of old railway cinder track and pleasant small roads. It is also suitable for the reasonably adventurous touring bike rider especially in dry weather. Likely muddy spots are: top of Madge Hill, the far end of Osmaston Park and Wigber Low. There are some fine views if you are blessed with clear weather.

Start in Ashbourne at the market square SK 181468. On a non-market day, if you are lucky, you may be able to park here. However it is often very busy so you may have to use one of the town's other carparks.

From the market square, facing the Town Hall, go left, then almost immediately left again, signposted 'St. Oswalds Hospital and Tissington Trail'. Curve right uphill before turning left on the road signposted 'Mapleton, Okeover, Tissington Trail'. Descend another 300 metres before going first right. This takes you onto the Tissington Trail (Cycle Hire and Tea). Ride along this flat disused railway for three and a half miles until the picnic site and carpark at Tissington (Tea/snacks shop).

Leave the trail here. The scenic village of Tissington (with a café!) is along the small road to your left. To continue the ride you need to turn right towards Bradbourne. Ignore the right turn to Basset Wood Farm and cycle a mile along this unfenced road before dropping very steeply to cross a slippery ford.

Cross the B5056 road with care then take the muddy track almost opposite (just right of the farm buildings). You will have to pass through a large metal gate before riding diagonally up the hill to the right. At the top of the hill, in the field, do not follow the right-hand wall as the track appears to, but go straight across to a large gate below dead trees, into a walled path. Consult your O.S. map here.

Go straight on after a small gate, through a gap/gateway in the next wall. Continue straight on, following the right-hand wall while contouring round Wigber Low. At another large gate go through and curve slightly to the left. Soon you will see Longrose Farm and a large barn (with a corrugated roof) ahead of you. You should also come to a large five-bar gate (just right of a water butt). Pass through this into the field in front of Longrose Farm.

Waterwheel, Osmaston Park

Beware - I got chased by about a dozen bullocks here! If you have similar problems shout loudly at them. Ride straight across the field to a footpath stile opposite. Do not go through it but follow along this side of the hedge to join a grassy hedged track. Pass top side of the riding stables through a narrow gap. Ride up their drive to meet a small road.

Turn right then after 250 metres turn first left through a large metal gate onto a small road/track. You should reach a larger road, the B5035 from Middleton. Go almost straight across and up the track opposite signposted 'Unsuitable For Motors'.

Bending to the right the track forks. Keep right and follow the track. After passing through two gates you will reach the top of the hill. A triangulation point sits in the field to your left. This unclassified road over Madge Hill offers fine views on clear days. Look for Carsington Reservoir, Thorpe Cloud, Dovedale and Ashbourne. Downhill from here the track gives way to a rutted field at the next gate. After this you join a semi-tarmacked track which you should follow steeply downhill, (being wary of cars on the blind bends!) to a T-junction and fingerpost.

Go left, signposted 'Bradley', and ride up this road for more than half a mile to the A517. Go straight across with great care (you are in a dip, hidden from cars, on a very fast road) following the sign marked 'Moorend/

Ednaston'. Follow this road through 'Hole in the Wall', a building with an arch-way over the road. Ignore the left turn (Hadly Lane). After about 400 metres the road curves sharply left (ignore Osmaston fork to your right).

A further 700 metres should bring you to a cross-roads with a small triangle of grass. Turn right here onto Rough Lane. After 200 metres you will come to a building. Follow the road as it bends ninety degrees left. A pleasant gated section of road takes you to the A52. Go left then next right signposted 'Shirley'.

As soon as you pass the village sign turn right (dead-end sign). Follow this road for roughly half a mile to a large gate. This bridleway becomes a gravel, then mud track which soon drops into Osmaston Park where a lake and water-wheel make a very pleasant spot to stop for a snack. After replenishment follow the bridleway straight up from the pond, ignoring the track right after 200 metres. At Osmaston (thatched cottages) go left and straight back into the park on the main tree lined drive (bridleway to Wyaston).

This soon forks right, then bends and goes over a cattlegrid. At the T-junction turn right and follow the waymarked gravel track down and up a large dip, through a gate (the left of the two) and down to some woods, passing a gravel parking spot. Go through two more wooden gates then up a grass field. Join the muddy hedged track to Wyaston Grange.

On meeting the road turn right, then right again after 600 metres, passing Wyaston Post Office. The second road left, about 400 metres beyond The Shirehorse Inn should be Wyaston Road which you need to follow until Ashbourne. You will meet a dead-end sign at the top of a steep hill. Go right to follow the one-way system and signs to Ashbourne centre.

In Ashbourne, at the five-way junction with traffic lights, turn right into the centre, past Sommerfields on your right. Turn right at the next traffic lights, ride under the Green Man/Black's Head pub sign, then fork left uphill.

This road leads back to the market square where you started.

*2002 No longer a café in Tissington or a Post Office in Wyaston.
If you wish to miss the delights of Ashbourne Town centre, it can now be bypassed by using the old railway tunnel which links the carpark near the Leisure Centre on Station Road to the starting point on the Tissington Trail.

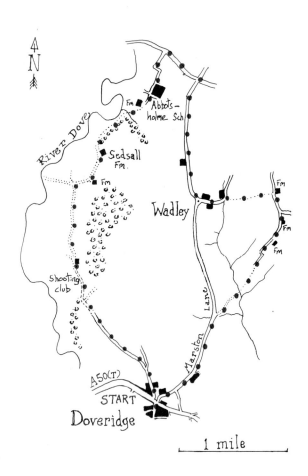

N

River Dove

Fm

Abbots-
holme Sch

Sedsall
Fm.

Fm

Wadley

Fm

Fm

Fm

Shooting
club

Marston Lane

A50(T)

START

Doveridge

1 mile

DOVERIDGE

Doveridge, Eaton Hall Farm, Abbotsholme School, Waldley, Marston Woodhouse Farm, Marston Lane, Doveridge Circle.

DISTANCE: 8 miles/13km (4mls/6¹/₂km on road)
TIME: 2 hours
MAPS: O.S. 1:25 000 Pathfinder: 831 - Uttoxeter sheet SK 03/13

A circuit through the rolling farmland on the Derbyshire Staffordshire border, skirting the plain of the River Dove which forms the county boundary. Beginning and ending in Doveridge it is a rich, subtle landscape of red brick farms, open fields and wooded hill slopes. You will see the massive JCB plant near Rocester, and in contrast, several impressive country houses. The riding is on a mixture of muddy tracks and small tarmac roads.

Start in Doveridge.There is parking on Park Crescent, near the Cavendish Arms, SK 116343. From the Cavendish Arms cross the A50(T) with care and go up Upswood Road which is almost opposite (in fact slightly left of) the pub. When this road forks, bear left. A good half mile will take you to a cattle grid where tarmac peters out and a track begins. When this track forks choose the left option signposted 'Staffs. Way".

This bridleway drops downhill to pass a pond and sport/shooting club and reach Eaton Hall Farm. Go through the gate on your left, (waymarked with a blue arrow) to pass just below the farm buildings. Do not curve sharp left again but instead go straight on through two large gates.

About half a mile along this good track (over fields) will bring you to a junction and four-way fingerpost. Turn right on the bridleway towards a brick farm signposted 'Bridleroad to Sedsall and Abbotsholme'. The track curves left before Eaton Dovedale Farm, but leads along to a splendid uninhabited brick farm (Sedsall Farm).

From here bear left on the track just below the farmhouse, signposted 'Staffs Way'. This muddy bridleway passes through a gate/gateway then after less than 250 metres go through another large gate. **The bridleway should leave the footpath here. However, on the ground it is difficult to follow the line of the bridleway shown on the O.S. map. Instead you will have to walk the Staffs. Way (footpath) for the next 400 metres.** To do this go straight down the field, pass through the large wooden gate, and curve right.

Follow this path for roughly 400 metres until you come to a small footbridge over a stream. Do not cross the bridge but turn right through a small gap in the fence. Cross an even smaller stream into Staffordshire where the line of the bridleway becomes footpath so please walk the next section. Pass through a rusty five-bar gate and up the narrow mud path between brambles.

Sedsall Farm

Turn right at the fork. You climb uphill parallel to the stream and soon come out on an open field **still walking.** Head straight across the field towards the farm. You should go through the large gate just right of Monk's Clownholm Farm, onto a hard track to Abbotsholme School.

You can now re-mount. Ride straight on, past the school (keeping the main building to your right) and along the tarmac drive in a north-easterly direction to a road. Turn right onto the road then take the first right (after less than half a mile) signposted 'Waldley and Doveridge'. Take the next left after a mile signposted 'Waldley and Marston'.

About 500 metres along this road, immediately after crossing Marston Brook, the road curves sharp left but you should leave it by going through the large gate in front of you and up the field. Follow the left-hand edge of the field, climbing to a bridlegate in the top corner. Pass through the gate and follow the right-hand edge of the field to a larger five-bar gate (the one straight in front of you, not the one on your right). Go through this and follow the line of hawthorns until it curves sharp right. At that point continue straight on across the field (beware of the shire horse) to Banktop Farm. Go through another gate and turn right onto the road.

This road curves sharply left. Leave the road by forking right, signposted 'Woodhouse Farm'. Pass the first farm and ride along the track. At the cattlegrid do not go down between the farm buildings but take the track right to follow the right-hand hawthorn hedge. Descend this muddy track, curving left then right. Go through the next gate and straight across to the far corner of the field where there is a stream.

There is a small footbridge and next to it a bridlegate, both leading onto a hedged track. Follow this hedged track. At the top of the track pass through a gate.

Turn left onto Marston Lane and ride straight back to the main road at Doveridge (ignoring a left turn to Sudbury). Cross the main road and go down Cook Lane beside the Cavendish Arms then right onto Park Crescent, your starting point.

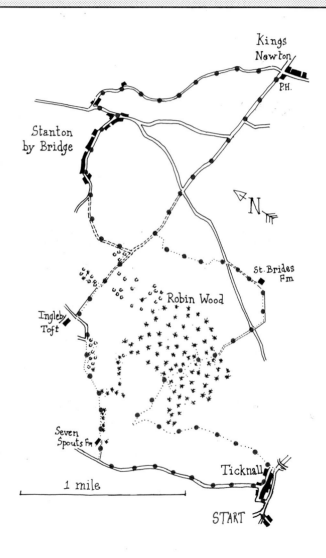

Kings
Newton

PH.

Stanton
by Bridge

N

St. Brides
Fm

Robin Wood

Ingleby
Toft

Seven
Spouts Fm

Ticknall

1 mile

START

TICKNALL/ROBIN WOOD

Ticknall, Robin Wood, Kings Newton, Stanton by Bridge, Ingleby Toft, Seven Spouts Farm, Ticknall Circle.

DISTANCE: $9^1/_2$ miles/15km (3mls/5km on road)
TIME: 3 hours
MAPS: O.S. 1:25 000 Pathfinder
852 - Burton on Trent sheet SK 22/32

The most southerly of the routes through arable farmland and woodland, bounded by the flood plain of the Trent in the north and the Leicestershire boundary in the south. The tracks are gravel, sand and mud. Some through ploughland can be heavy in wet weather. There are some fine estates and houses (Calke Abbey is worth a visit) as well as some traditional farmhouses along the way.

Start in the public carpark at Ticknall Village Hall on Ingleby Lane SK 352240. Turn right out of the carpark and take the next left, Chapel Street. Ride about 200 metres along the tarmac to meet a large gate. Go through the gap beside the gate onto the grassed area, then turn immediately left through the bridlegate onto a field.

Ride straight across this field to a bridlegate opposite. Pass through this and struggle across two large ploughed fields to another bridlegate. After this gate follow the left edge of the field, pass through another small gate then cut across the corner of the next field towards the edge of Robin Wood. Enter the plantation via a wooden bridlegate, cycle along a short stretch of path deep in pine needles, then exit via a gate.

Go straight across the field. On reaching a hedge with a stile in it, turn right. Follow the track, at first alongside the hedge then curving left through a gap in it. This takes you into another field. Cut the right-hand corner of the field and re-enter Robin Wood through a small bridlegate. Follow the good track through the woods. When you meet a large gravel 'forestry type' track do not turn left but join it and go straight on. Another bridlegate will take you out of the woods onto a well-surfaced track. Four hundred metres along this you will meet a road.

Cross directly over it into the field opposite. Ride along the field boundary which soon curves sharply left down to St. Bride's Farm. Turn left to follow the track above the farm buildings back to the road. Cross the road again onto the bridleway opposite. This bridleway, a sandy track with some puddles, is quite well defined on the ground. It crosses four fields then comes to a T-junction with a tarmac drive. If you have any problems following it, have a look at your O.S. map. At the T-junction go right and follow the tarmac for 500 metres to a cross-roads. Cross the road and ride down Breach Lane opposite.

You will meet the B587 (Derby Road) in less than half a mile. Turn right (technically straight on). After only 200 metres, when the road curves sharply right, go straight on following the signs 'Kings Newton, Isley Walton and E. Midlands Airport'. Less than half a mile along this road you will enter the village of King's Newton and should take the track left opposite Ye Olde Packhorse Inn, signposted 'Holywell'. Follow this track for roughly a mile, ignoring all turn-offs. You will come to the road at Stanton by Bridge. Turn left, then first right after only 200 metres.

Alternative Start/Finish point A. SK 373272, see page 25

Ride up this road for about half a mile. Once past all the houses the road soon curves sharply right and a wide farm track (unclassified road) forks left. Take the farm track and pass under the large electricity power lines. Less than half a mile of this well-surfaced track will take you to a large metal gate.

Go through the gate, turn right, pass Woodhead Cottages and descend on the muddy bridleway before climbing to a small road by Ingleby Toft.

At the road turn left. After a mere 200 metres, when the road curves sharply right leave the tarmac by riding straight on through a gateway and along a track. You are now on the bridleway to Seven Spouts Farm. Follow the track along the wood's edge ignoring several tracks that break off left. Pass a pond, then at the farm go left up the tarmac drive. This drive winds round to meet the road. Cut the corner by leaving the drive at the first sharp right bend and pass through the large gate onto the same road. Turn left and ride nearly a mile on tarmac to finish back in Ticknall.

STARTING EITHER OF THE TWO TICKNALL ROUTES FROM DERBY
Ticknall/Robin Wood and Ticknall/Repton Shrubs Circles can be joined at several different points by riding from Derby on the cycleway. See the notes in the route descriptions and the instructions in the Trails and Cycleways section, under DERBY CYCLEWAY headings.

Kings Newton

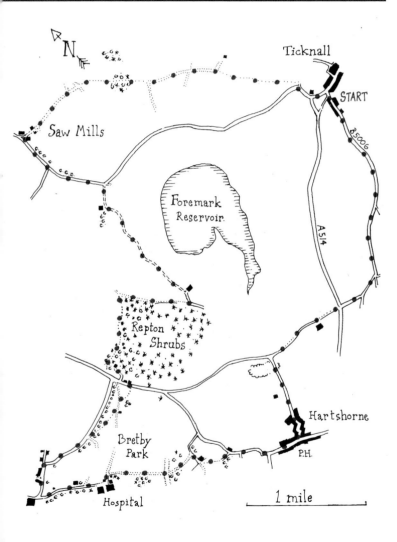

N

Ticknall

START

B5006

A514

Saw Mills

Foremark Reservoir

Repton Shrubs

Hartshorne

P.H.

Bretby Park

Hospital

1 mile

TICKNALL/REPTON SHRUBS

Ticknall, Saw Mill (Milton), Repton Common, Repton Shrubs, Bretby, Bretby Hall, Hartshorne, Ticknall Circle.

DISTANCE: 14 miles/22km (7mls/11km on road)
TIME: 4 hours
MAPS: O.S. 1:25 000 Pathfinder
852- Burton on Trent sheet SK 22/32

This route, in the south-western corner of Derbyshire, skirts the historic town of Repton and passes Foremark Reservoir. It is rich farming country, a landscape of hedges, open parkland and small woods. The tracks are a mixture of sand and mud. Some can be heavy going if wet.

Start in the public carpark at Ticknall Village Hall on Ingleby Lane. Turn right out of the carpark and down to the main street, turn right along the A514 and take the right turn signposted 'Foremark, Errwood Reservoir'. On the first left-hand corner after only 200 metres, a waymarked bridleway leaves the road to the right. Take this by going through the large gate then follow the left-hand edge of the next five fields, passing through large gates as necessary.

You should come to a small wooden bridlegate. This takes you onto the sixth field. Follow the right-hand hedge straight on to join a larger track. Along this track is a junction with a track forking left. Ignore the track left and ride straight on, to pass under the large overhead powerlines. You will soon meet a wooden bridlegate, the entrance to a small wood.

Ride down through the wood and out via a gate at the bottom. Follow the left edge of the next field round to a large gate, then into a hedged track. Descend this vehicle-rutted track into an open farmyard (Saw Mills); go through a gateway and up to a road. Turn left and follow this road for three quarters of a mile (ignoring the road right to Lawn Bridge) until a sandy, well-drained track with a dead-end sign leaves the road to the right. Take this track, pass Brookdale Farm, go through a large metal gate and climb steadily.

The area to your left is Repton Common. You will soon get a good view of Foremark Reservoir. On reaching the large gate at the top of the track go through the gap beside it and turn right onto tarmac. Waste Farm is to your left.

After only 200 metres turn sharp right again, on a track down the edge of a plantation (Repton Shrubs). Descend for half a mile. At the bottom corner of the wood go left, almost doubling back on yourself. As you enter the wood you will meet the corner of another track. Stay on the bridleway closest to the fields on your right. Do not take any tracks deeper into the wood. The bridleway you are on will probably be very muddy and hard going.

Heading towards Repton Shrubs

There is a good downhill section. Then, just before meeting the stream, take the path that turns ninety degrees left uphill. It passes immediately below Cherry Tree Cottage. Ride down the drive, curving to the right to join the road. Go left onto the road but then right through a bridlegate after only 300 metres. The bridlegate is just before a pond.

Head back right across this field to cross a farm track by two gates. Head up the field, pass just below the three large trees and join the indistinct path that contours round to a bridlegate. After passing through this gate ride down through the woods to a metal gate. Turn right here to join the road then go left up to Bretby.

Follow the road as it curves left signposted 'Bretby Hospital and Swadlincote'. Take the next left turn; the drive to Bretby Hall Hospital. Go up the drive, then at the hospital buildings take the first track left opposite the boiler room. Skirt the small wood by curving sharply right just before the large gate.

Descend the well-compacted track, pass between two ponds and ride straight on uphill. At the brow you will cross what appears to be some kind of equestrian race track before dropping down a muddy track into Hoofies Wood; at the bottom turn right. Ride along past Hoofies Farm.

Pass through the metal gate into the field. Head downhill, slightly to the left and go through the large gate. Follow the left edge of the field. Ride down the path, cross the stream, then up a short climb to the road and turn right. In Hartshorne turn left opposite the Chesterfield Arms pub up Brook Street. Climb steadily for half a mile. At the hilltop turn right on a track which leaves the road on a left-hand bend. This track along Gravelpit Hill may be wet but should not be muddy. Follow it for half a mile.

Pass The Buildings Farm and come out at a road junction. Go straight across, up the tarmac road opposite. After a good half mile take the first left turn signposted 'Derby and Ticknall'.

This is the B5006 road. Follow it back to your starting point at Ticknall!

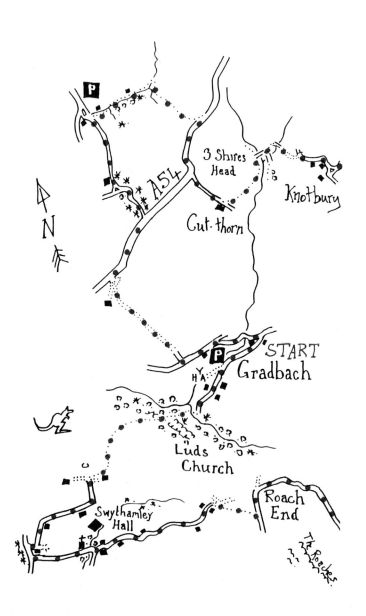

P

N

A54

3 Shires
Head

Knotbury

Cut·thorn

START
P
H Y A
Gradbach

Luds
Church

Swythamley
Hall

Roach
End

The Roaches

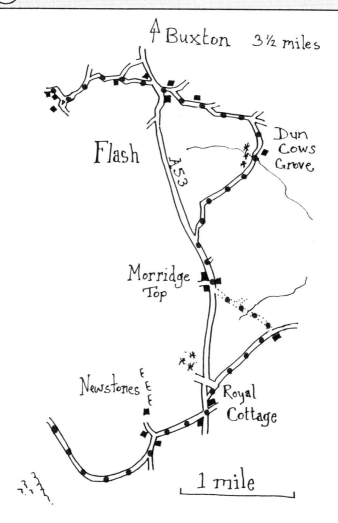

↟ Buxton   3½ miles

Dun Cows Grove

Flash

A53

Morridge Top

Newstones

Royal Cottage

1 mile

GRADBACH

Gradbach, Lud's Church, Danebridge, Hillylees, Roach End, Hazel Barrow, Dun Cows Grove, Flash Bar, Knotbury, Three Shires Head, Danethorn Hollow, Wildboarclough, Tagsclough Hill, Gradbach.

DISTANCE:	23 miles/36.8km (13mls/20.8km on road)
TIME:	4 hours
MAPS:	O.S. 1:25 000 Outdoor Leisure: 24-White Peak (west)

This is a gritstone flavoured route with high moorlands, sandy tracks and fine views, based around the crags and rocky outcrops of The Roaches. It is unashamedly hilly as it dips and climbs in and out of various cloughs with many tributaries to the river Dane. Although there is a fair amount of road riding, traffic is generally very light on most stretches and it is well worth it as you stray from Derbyshire into Staffordshire and Cheshire too. As you pass through the small mixed woodlands watch out for lurking wallabies!

Start at the Peak National Carpark at Gradbach SK 999662. Leave the carpark by turning right and follow the tarmac road, ignoring the right fork to Gradbach Youth Hostel. You will climb slightly to a cluster of houses (Gradbach itself). Continue on the obvious track as tarmac gives way to a sand and stone surface, ignoring any turn-offs. This walled track drops into Gradbach Wood to a large gate with a concessionary bridleway sign and white arrow. Pass through the smaller gate to ford Black Brook and bear right uphill towards Lud's church, signed 'Swythamley'. Follow this very pleasant path with a very rideable sand and pine-needle surface through oak, pine and birch woodland to a clearing beside a small gritstone outcrop.

The footpath left leads to Lud's church. You could leave your bike locked here and walk up to this small, dramatic gorge thought to be one of the settings mentioned in 'Gawain and the Green Knight'.

From the clearing continue straight on, out of the woodland and across moorland with bilberry and heather, then through a large gate, downhill to a fingerpost and second gate. You will be able to see the ridges of the Roaches to your left. Continue through the gate (signed 'bridleway' and 'Danebridge') until another junction and gate. Take the track downhill, leaving the prominent Hanging Stone behind you. This soon curves ninety degrees right then becomes tarmac at Park House (with a large outside wall lamp). Ride straight on to the T-junction opposite West Lodge. Turn right, then after 40 metres turn left at a second T-junction. Ignore a road that falls off to the right and curve left on the flat 'parkland' road. Pass a stone church and ride over a bridge then turn immediately left past Hillylees Farm. This little-used road is lined with mature oak, ash, sycamore and lime trees. It climbs steadily for a good mile towards the Roaches.

After passing a farm you will reach two large gates where a track curves sharp left. One gate says 'Private, No Public Access'. You want the other gate on the right. It leads into a field on an indistinct grass track (an unclassified road, no longer walled on the left as the map shows). It is flat and stays close to the right hand wall until a boggy patch and a DIY gate (re-build it every time you use it!). Go through this, continue on until you meet tarmac and turn sharp left uphill until the 407m spot height where you should get great views.

Stay on this road as it contours round below the Roaches then swoops down and round to the left (ignore a road from the right) to a T-junction. Turn right. At the A53 turn left then right after only 200 metres signed Longnor. After cycling a good half mile take the track left opposite the houses (Ridge Head) marked 'Unsuitable For Motors'. This hard track soon crosses a brook which could cause large muddy patches in winter. Keep left at the track junction then right on meeting the A53. After less than half a mile on this busy road take the second right marked 'Unsuitable for Heavy Goods Vehicles'. A great downhill drops you into Dun Cow's Grove but a steep climb follows to a junction. Turn left. It is uphill to meet the A53 again at Flash Bar Stores.

Flash claims to be England's highest village, standing at just over fifteen hundred feet. It sits just below Axe Edge (the long gritstone escarpment that the busy A53 runs along) and Axe Moor, a high exposed place which gets over four feet of rain a year and is the source of five rivers - the Dove, Manifold, Wye, Goyt and Dane (that's some sponge!).

Turn right then immediately left. Ride downhill for roughly three quarters of a mile until a road junction with a large grass triangle. Go right here uphill on the road marked 'Dead End Except for Access'. Follow the tarmac until its demise, at a large gate. Drop ninety degrees left on a stony walled track until a gate and impressive small stone bridge over a stream. Cross the bridge and head left on a tricky rocky stretch, rideable only with care, through the next gate to come out at Three Shires Head.

This is a beautiful little spot with two pack horse bridges where two streams meet to form the River Dane. The streams form the borders of Derbyshire, Staffordshire and Cheshire. On a hot day a waterfall and the Pannier pool make a good paddling and picnic spot. Until the end of the nineteenth century this spot attracted all sorts of rogues who would cross back and forward between counties to avoid the authorities.

Pass straight across the bridge and bear left on the slightly difficult track which climbs up and round to meet a road at Cut Thorn. Turn right and continue uphill to the A54. Go right again but after less than half a mile turn left opposite the start of the crash barriers on a track marked 'No cars except for access'. After the gate this enjoyable bit of track soon descends, curving sharp left to cross Cumberland Brook by a waterfall. It is downhill parallel to a wood with rowan and scots pine. Re-ford the stream then meet

a road at Clough House. Turn left, ignore a road right to Wildboarclough, and climb up this road shaded by larch, beech and rhododendron until a T-junction. Turn right onto the A54 for half a mile. Look for the first track left which doubles back uphill. It has a large metal gate, with 'Heild End Farm', and 'No Car Access' signs.

Ride up here curving sharp right then forking left, then round the hill climbing less steeply. The surface is good as is the view of Gradbach Hill ahead. Pass through the next three gates as you descend. At the fourth ignore the track just before it and take the walled lane straight on to a road. Turn left and descend all the way to cross the river Dane and enter Staffordshire. After only about 300 metres take the track right marked Gradbach Youth Hostel and follow the road back to your starting point.

Ford at Cumberland Brook

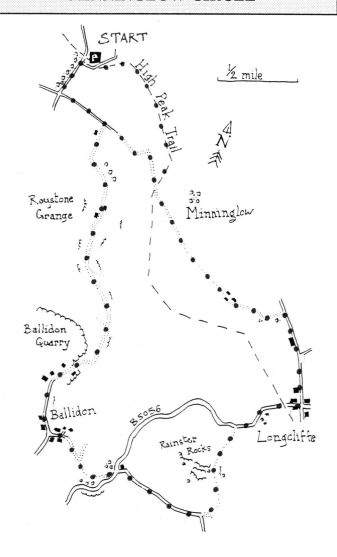

START

High Peak Trail

½ mile

N

Minninglow

Roystone Grange

Ballidon Quarry

Ballidon

B5056

Rainster Rocks

Longcliffe

MINNINGLOW CIRCLE

Minninglow carpark, Roystone Grange, Ballidon, Rainster Rocks, Longcliffe, Minninglow Hill, Roystone.

DISTANCE: 8 miles/12.8km (2mls/3.2km on road)
TIME: 2 hours
MAPS: O.S. 1:25 000 Outdoor Leisure: 24-White Peak (east)

This short limestone route passes through a quiet dry limestone dale where monks had a large sheep farm in the 12th century. Today the sheep are still there but not the monks. A large working limestone quarry, the High Peak Trail (a disused railway line) and a bronze age burial mound all add to the variety of what is basically upland limestone farming country where the soil is thin and any flattish areas are grazed. The trees are rather sparse, ash and hawthorn being some of the hardy survivors although there are some planted shelter belts. The surfaces are mixed - about half hard track and half grass which can get muddy but almost no road work. This short but hilly route makes a good evening or morning ride with plenty of trails nearby for those with more time to cycle further, or walk.

Start at Minninglow carpark (High Peak Trail) SK 194582. Turn right out of the carpark and turn left to head south on Parwich Lane for only 500 metres before turning left again. Ride downhill and take the first track right. This leads down through Roystone Grange in the bottom of an imposing dry limestone dale. You will pass through the yard of a working farm and then pass just left of an old pumphouse.

This pumphouse housed a large water-cooled engine in the nineteenth century, used to pump compressed air through cast iron pipes (scary stuff!) to drive rock drills in the nearby quarries that sprung up along the High Peak Trail. It is built on the original site of a 12th century monastic sheep farm which exported wool to Europe.

After a further half mile you will emerge in the huge, working Ballidon quarry. Ride straight on through the works taking care to watch out for large lorries and other machinery. Soon after re-joining tarmac, take the first left to climb past Cow Close Farm. Ignore a drive to the left, cross the cattlegrid and continue uphill until a sharp left-hand corner. Leave the well-surfaced track here by passing through the large wooden gate (you may have to unhook and re-attach a makeshift fence).

Climb slightly following the old grass track before dropping down and round the hill, then zig-zagging to another large gate. Cross the B5056 with care and go straight up the lane opposite. It is half a mile before this road curves sharp right. At this point turn left through a small bridlegate with the imposing limestone outcrop of Rainster Rocks ahead of you, to the left. The following short section of bridleway is mainly grass so can prove soft

Katie. Minninglow

going in wet weather. The path heads over to the corner of a wall just right of the rocks. You should follow the left hand wall to a bridlegate, then cross sides so that you keep the wall to your right.

Climb straight on, past a barn, to the road. Go right, uphill. You will soon pass under the High Peak Trail and should then take the next road left signed 'Aldwark'. After nearly half a mile you will pass a large farm on your left with lots of lorries. After two more fields on your left, take the wide track left. Negotiate a makeshift gate after only 100 metres and follow the track which soon bears right to a farm. Go through the yard of the farm and a large gate, then past the snarling (but, hopefully, chained) dogs. Ride along the narrow field to and through another large gate. From here basically head straight on! You should first follow the left-hand wall until it curves left, then go straight on until there is a wall on your right. Follow this to the next gateway.

To your right you will see Minninglow, an ancient burial mound topped by a clump of wind-blown beech trees which, along with its height, make it such a distinctive sight from so many places in the Peak District. Here Neolithic tribes constructed 'big stone' chambered tombs to communally bury their dead.

After this gate follow the left-hand wall. Riding straight on through the next three large wooden five-bar gates and down the wide walled lane (which may be muddy) should bring you to the High Peak Trail.

From here are two options:

A. Turn right and follow the trail just over half a mile back to your start point.
or

B. Go straight across the trail, through the large gate to continue down the walled lane. It descends for 500 metres then curves left. Follow this track uphill (ignoring the tracks right) until you pass a point you should recognise from earlier in your ride and reach the Parwich road. Turn right, then first right again, back to your starting point.

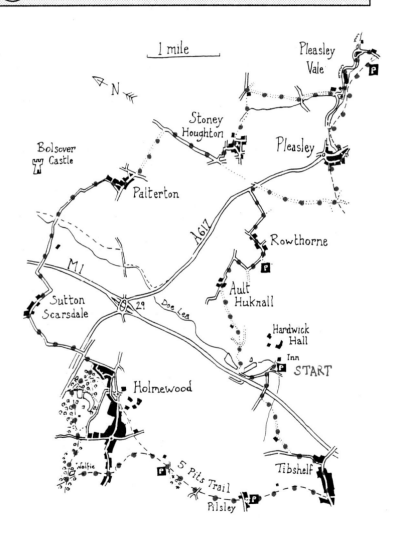

1 mile

N

Pleasley
Vale

Stoney
Houghton

Pleasley

Bolsover
Castle

Palterton

A617

Rowthorne

M1

Ault
Huknall

Sutton
Scarsdale

29

Doe Lea

Hardwick
Hall

Inn
START

Holmewood

Wolfie

5 Pits Trail

Tibshelf

Pilsley

BOLSOVER

Hardwick Inn, Tibshelf, Five Pits Trail, Holmewood, Sutton Scarsdale, Palterton, Stoney Houghton, Pleasley, Rowthorne, Ault Hucknall, Hardwick Hall.

DISTANCE: 25 miles/40km (13mls/21km on road)
TIME: 3¹/₂ hours
MAPS: O.S. 1:50 000 Landranger sheet:
120 - Mansfield and Worksop

Easily accessible from junction 29 of the M1, this route takes you through the industrial coalfields of north-east Derbyshire. Cycling on abandoned railway lines and green lanes, you pass by old mining villages, opencast coal sites and reclaimed spoil heaps as well as large country houses financed from the profits of the mining industry. There is even a choice of 16th century inn or miners welfare club for a dinner stop. A rolling route that is all rideable.

Start at the carpark just before the Hardwick Inn SK 457633. Turn left out of the carpark, right, then left again towards Hardstoft. Cross over the M1 and after only a few hundred metres take the first track left. Hedged and initially downhill, after crossing a stream it narrows and climbs between two fields of crops. The path soon becomes a track again, passes Biggin Farm and meets a road. Turn left, then next right at the White Hart, heading into Tibshelf.

Continue until you see the Wheatsheaf Pub on your left. Turn left down Station Road, just after the pub and turn left again to head north back under the road on the Five Pits Trail (an old railway line). You will follow this undulating trail for the next three miles to Holmewood. Follow the trail, crossing two roads until you reach Timber Lane. Turn right onto tarmac (briefly) then left back onto the trail.

When the trail forks go left signed Grassmoor, follow the trail turning left then right to meet the A6175. The Five Pits Trail continues across the road to Wolfie pond. Turn right around the pond signed Williamthorpe. This leads under the Chesterfield Road to a junction. Keep straight on, passing the remains of Williamthorpe Colliery and Williamthorpe Ponds. Cross Muster Brook and head uphill to another junction. Continue straight on until a track can be seen heading towards the left end of the houses. Follow this to appear on Slack Lane next to the last house. Turn left. At the next junction turn right then almost immediately left and ride to Sutton Scarsdale where you should turn right towards Palterton. You will cross the M1 again. As you climb into Palterton curve right staying on the larger road then left up Main Street. Ignore a left to Bolsover. Continue until the next road junction.

Here ride straight across onto a hedged track with bridleway fingerpost. This is a great little rural grass track, banked and hedged high on both

Pleasley Pit

sides mainly with elder and elm. At the road turn right then after half a mile take the left at a small cross-roads. After 300 metres turn sharp right. As you descend into Stoney Houghton, pass the large farms but look for the first track left (when the road bends sharp right). Go left here, pass the lovely derelict farm with a red tile roof and follow the narrow, winding single-track that may be overgrown with nettles through woods and ford a stream. The path becomes wider and climbs slightly to a small road. Turn right, not on the road but on the right of the two tracks. It hugs the edge of the electricity sub-station. This wide, bumpier track is the 'Archeaological Trail'.

After nearly a mile cross a small road and take the narrow but hard-surfaced path to Pleasley Vale. You will emerge at the back of a metal engineering works. At the road turn left. Avoid the automatically triggered barriers that have been known to spring to life and knock cyclists off and ride through Pleasley Vale past the mills (which are being renovated).

Continue on this road, past a war memorial, and climbing uphill. After you pass a derelict warehouse look for a small carpark on your right. Pass under the height restriction barrier, through the carpark and onto the Meden Trail. Follow this disused railway line until a steep descent. Turn left at the bottom. Pass under the A617 adjacent the River Meden. A very short section of footpath leads to the Chesterfield road. Turn right riding uphill past the

Nags Head and along until you see a roundabout. Turn left just before the roundabout onto Pit Lane.

Follow this until you see a horse & kissing gate on your left. Turn left through the gate and right to follow the old railway line for half a mile, where you climb onto a banked junction and should turn right. This wide track skirts the edge of the land reclamation work. To your right you will see the old very imposing headstocks and engine houses of Pleasley Pit.

The old Pleasley is notable for a number of reasons. At 2,800ft it was the deepest mine in the east midlands coalfield and the first 'deep mine' in the area. It was the first mine to use the distinctive steel headstocks and the winding gear was powered by two huge steam engines, which although dormant are still more or less intact. Pleasley is the only Derbyshire colliery left that still has its headstocks and winding gear.

Continue along this track about a mile until you meet a road. Go left, then left again until a T-junction. Turn left here through Rowthorn. Follow the road past Rowthorn Trail. Curve sharp right. At the T-junction turn left signposted 'Hardwick Hall'. In Ault Hucknall, look for a track left just after passing the graveyard. This track takes you to a very impressive grey bridlegate. Go through this into the grounds of Hardwick Hall.

Descend on grass following the crest of the ridge, staying reasonably close to the right-hand fence, past a waymark post then cross the tarmac track at the elbow of its corner. Go through the small bridlegate and cross diagonally left over the field towards the bottom left-hand corner and the ponds. At the track turn right, past the carpark (unless you want to stop and leave your bike for a walk around). At the road turn left back to your start point!

*2002 The warehouse opposite the carpark is no longer derelict.
The wide track, which skirts the edge of the Pleasley Pit site, is the lower of two parallel tracks.

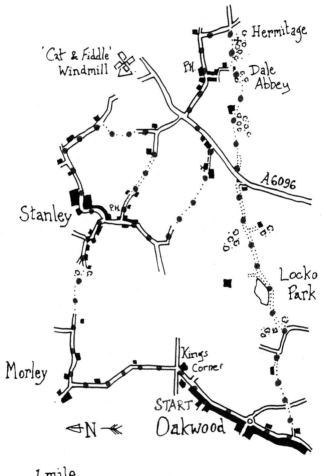

'Cat & Fiddle' Windmill

Hermitage

P.H.

Dale Abbey

A6096

Stanley

P.H.

Locko Park

Morley

Kings Corner

START
Oakwood

◁N◁

1 mile

LOCKO PARK

Oakwood, Locko Park, Dunnshill, Dale Abbey, The Flourish, Stanley, Hagg Farms, Stanley, Morley, Oakwood.

DISTANCE: 12 miles/19.2km (5mls/8km on road)
TIME: 2¹/₂ hours
MAPS: O.S. 1:50 000 Landrangers Nos 128 and 129

This ride, between Derby and Ilkeston on the edge of the ever expanding Oakwood estate is a real charmer, gently sauntering through wooded parkland and hedged green lanes and across open fields. Every second building seems to be a large brick farm with a handful of stables and horses to match. It is easy to follow and isn't hilly. The surfaces are mixed but generally good and there are pleasant small woods with mature oak, lime, beech and hazel coppices. You will pass a Hermit's Cave, an old ruined Abbey and spot the Cat and Fiddle windmill. There is a choice of pubs for refreshment. It is an ideal family or evening ride. You will probably meet horse riders; the horses seem very skittish around cycles so slow down and pass wide or stop and let them pass.

Park on Smalley Drive in Oakwood SK 3939. Ride east to Morley Road, turn right, ride down to a roundabout and go straight across. After roughly 600 metres look for a track on your left signposted 'BR No.10 to Locko Park' and 'Morley Road Nos. 136-142'. Turn left up here. It is easy to follow. Cross the first road you meet but at the second turn right. At the next bend take the bridleway left into Locko Park, a metalled drive through park gates. Pass a fruit farm and the large lake on your left. This is a really plush tree-lined parkland drive. Fork next right, still on tarmac, until the surface becomes gravel and there is another split. Go straight on through the gate. The next sandy stretch is a little like riding on the beach!

After the next gate continue straight ahead to cross the road and follow the narrower waymarked path. After a further gate the track becomes wider and gravelly. It soon curves topside of a brick farm, to a gate into a field of cattle. Cross to, but not through the large gateway. Instead follow the top side of the hedge, on a path that leads to a large metal gate. Continue on the obvious track through a pleasant mixed woodland, through gates as necessary to reach a smaller gate in front of a house. Turn right through the stable yard and follow the path through Hermits Wood, then across an open field to a road.

At the road turn left, follow it as it curves sharp left and passes the Carpenters Arms pub in Dale Abbey (a prime spot for a little refreshment?). If you want to look around the village it is down to your left. To continue your route, ride along to the A6096 and turn left. After half a mile take a track right by a bus-stop (signs for 'Hollies Farm' and 'Antiques'). This

The entrance to Locko Park

crosses a cattlegrid and leads to another large farm with horse stables. Follow the track between the buildings with the garden of the house to your left. Curve left following the track which crosses under the electricity lines very close to the large metal pylon. You should find a waymarked bridlegate. Ride the marked track across several open fields to a gravel track and subsequently along to a road.

At the road turn right. Take the next right too, just before the Bridge Inn, marked as a dead end. Follow tarmac along until it falters at Meadow Farm. Ride straight on through the ubiquitous gates to pass an attractive brick farm. At the next buildings, Upper Hagg Farm, turn left (red waymarking arrow and fingerpost), skirting below the brick stables to follow the hedged track downhill. Turn left at the road towards Stanley. Pass through the village but turn right onto Morley Lane just before The White Hart. At the fork go left. You will rise slightly to cross the old (now tree-covered) railway line then turn left on a narrow path between a bench and a small garage (The Midshires Way). This drops to ford a small stream, climbs up a field onto a track, then soon re-joins tarmac where you should continue straight on.

Turn left at the next T-junction, then straight on at the crossroads. Turn right after a short distance, back onto Smalley Drive where you started.

USEFUL ADDRESSES

* When writing to any organisation do not forget to include a SAE.

LOCAL/REGIONAL ADDRESSES

D.C.C. Derbyshire County Council,
County Offices, Matlock, Derbyshire DE4 3AG.Tel. 01629 580000

Staffordshire County Council,
Planning and Development Office, Martin Street, Stafford ST16 2LE. Tel. 01785 223121

Cheshire County Council
Public Rights of Way, Goldsmith House, Hamilton Place, Chester CH1 1SE. Tel. 01244 662424

Nottingham County Council
Public Rights of Way, Trent Bridge House, Fox Road, West Bridgeford, Nottingham NG2 6BJ

Derbyshire Countryside Services (Rangers):

Central Area, Middleton Top Visitor Centre, Middleton-by-Wirksworth, Derbyshire. Tel. 01629 823204

High Peak Junction Visitor Centre. Tel. 01629 822831

North Eastern Area, Clay Cross Countryside Centre, 23 Market Street, Clay Cross, S45 9JE. Tel. 01246 866960

East Area, Shipley Country Park, The Visitor Centre,Slack Lane, Heanor, Derbyshire DE7 7GX. Tel. 01773 719961

Derbyshire Public Transport Infomation. Tel. 01332 292200

Peak National Park, Aldern House, Baslow Road, Bakewell, Derbyshire DE45' 1AE. Tel. 01629 814321

Peak National Park Study Centre, Lose Hill Hall, Castleton, Derbyshire S30 2WB. Tel. 01433 620373

Peak Park Information Centres
Bakewell	01629 813227
Castleton	01433 20679
Edale	01433 70207
Fairholmes (Derwent Valley)	01433 50953
Hartington Old Signal Box	
Torside (Longdendale Valley)	

D.C.C./PEAK PARK CYCLE HIRE CENTRES

Telephone Numbers:

Hayfield	01663 746222
Ashbourne	01335 343156
Middleton Top	01629 823204
Waterhouses	01538 308609
Parsley Hay	01298 84493
Derwent	01433 65161

Dirt Tracks, Hope Valley Bike Hire (Hathersage) 01433 650199

NATIONAL ORGANISATIONS

Ordnance Survey, Romsey Road,Southampton SO16 4GU. Tel. 01703 792000

Countryside Commission Headquarters, John Dower House, Crescent Place,Cheltenham,Gloucester GL50 3PA. Tel. 01242 521381

Midlands Regional Office, 1st Floor, Vincent House, Tindal Bridge, 92-93 Edward Street, Birmingham B1 2RA. Tel. 0121 2339399

Department of Transport Headquarters, Great Minster House, 76 Marsham Street, London SW1P 4DR. Tel. 0171 271 5000

British Waterways Headquarters, Willow Grange, Church Road, Watford, Hertfordshire WD1 3QA. Tel. 01923 226422

YHA National Office, YHA, Trevelyan House, 8 St. Stephen's Hill, St Albans, Hertfordshire AL1 2DY. Tel. 01727 855215

YHA Regional Office, YHA Northern England, PO Box 11, Matlock, Derbyshire DE4 2XA. Tel. 01629 825850

CYCLING ORGANISATIONS

British Cycling Federation and British Mountain Bike Federation, National Cycling Centre, Stuart Street, Manchester M11 49Q. Tel. 0161 2302301

British Cycle Cross Association, 14 Dene Side Road, Darlington, County Durham DL3 9HZ. Tel. 01325 482052

Association of Lightweight Campers, Mrs B. Palmer (Section Sec.), 31 Bowbridge Lock, London Road, Stroud, Glos. GL5 2JZ. Tel. 01453 755993

The Tandem Club, Box TC, CTC, 69 Meadrow,Goldalming, Surrey GU7 3HS

The Tandem Club, Membership Secretary, Lynda Fargher, Tandem Club, 5 Sewards Club, Wickford, Essex SS12 9PB

CTC Cycle Touring Club, Cotterell House, 69 Meadrow, Godalming, Surrey GU7 3HS. Tel. 01483 417217

Rough Stuff Fellowship, Membership Details, 12 Avondale Road, Edgeley, Stockport SK3 9NX

Trailquest League Information Line, S.A.E. to Trail Cyclists Association, Coddington, Ledbury HR8 1JH

ACCESS / CONSERVATION / CAMPAIGN ORGANISATIONS

Sustrans, 35 King Street, Bristol B51 4DZ. Tel. 0117 9268893

BTCV Head Office, 36 St. Mary's St., Wallingford, Oxon OX10 0EU

Trans-Pennine Officer, Pam Ashton, c/o Department of Planning, Barnsley Metropolitan Borough Council, Central Offices, Kendray Street, Barnsley S70 2TN

Open Spaces Society, 25a Bell Street, Henley-on-Thames, Oxfordshire RG9 2BA. Tel. 01491 573535

The National Trust, 36 Queen Anne's Gate, London SW1H 9AS. Tel. 0171 222 9251

Friends of the Earth, 26-8 Underwood Street, London N1 7JQ. Tel. 0171 490 1555

Green Party, 1A Waterloo Road, London N19 5NJ. Tel. 0171 272 4474

ITDG, Intermediate Technology Development Group, Myson House, Railway Terrace, Rugby CV21 3HT. Tel. 01788 560631

PUBLIC TRANSPORT IN DERBYSHIRE

For Bus, Coach and Train times – www.derbybus.net or ring Trvaveline 0870 608 2 608

NOTES

NOTES

NOTES

The Lake District, The Howgills & The Yorkshire Dales

JEREMY ASHCROFT

36 selected routes amongst England's finest mountains; some completely new, some established classics.

All levels of ability catered for - routes across summits, passes, moorland, & along valleys.

Each route lavishly illustrated with freshly drawn maps in 2 colours, and b&w photos depicting the variety of terrain and weather conditions.

Clearly written route descriptions. Guidance on equipment, mountain survival and access & conservation.

ISBN 0 948153-10-5 **£7.50**

Breaking Loose

DAVE COOK

'The mass of men lead live of quiet desperation', and few realise their dreams of escape. Dave Cook followed his dream and in 1989 set off for Australia on his bicycle. His vivid account tells of rock-climbing adventures en route, of friends made and of the political situations he found - including a tangle with Saddam Hussein's police. Throughout he records with keen observation and refreshing honesty his reflections on social injustice from Yugoslavia to the Indian continent; and on his own moral values and the pursuit of dreams.

ISBN 0 948153-26-1 **£9.50**

To order by mail, send a cheque made out to THE ERNEST PRESS adding 10% for post & packing.
THE ERNEST PRESS, LOCHABER, LLANFAELOG, ANGLESEY LL63 5TS.

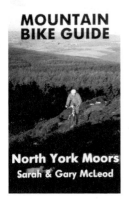

North York Moors

SARAH & GARY McLEOD

20 well-researched and legal routes over the open space of the North York Moors. Careful attention to conservation permeates the text with sites of potential erosion highlighted. All routes are clearly described and illustrated with two-colour maps and numerous photographs.

The guide caters well for family days but points out longer days through route linking for the young and fit.

ISBN 0 948153-30-X

£6.95

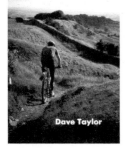

The Midlands

DAVE TAYLOR

This is the Mountain Bike Guide - family edition. The pages are packed with routes for fun days out or peaceful summer evenings in beautiful countryside.

But, Hammerheads, do not dismay! There are plenty of punishing climbs and the potential for some long, challenging days out.

Each of the 21 routes is illustrated with black and white photos and includes a two-colour sketch-map, local history etc.

ISBN 0 948153-29-6

£6.95

Kent

GARY TOMPSETT

21 well-researched circular routes throughout Kent - the garden of England. Discover this intricate county using the carefully drawn sketch-maps and clearly written route descriptions. Each route is accompanied by an unusual wealth of information on local history and geography, attractions and off route amenities and access rights. Black and white illustrations show the rich variety of landscapes visited. There are routes for all abilities, between 5 and 50 km, providing an essential guide for all off road cyclists. Beginners, families and expert riders will delight in the variety on offer. Just jump on your bike and go.

ISBN 0 94815-34-2

£6.95

More routes in The Lakes, Howgills & The Yorkshire Dales

JEREMY ASHCROFT

Due to the great demand from the author's first Mountain Bike Guide to the Lakes, Howgills and Yorkshire Dales, this second book has been compiled. Using the same format with superb two-colour maps and clear route descriptions, this second group of 36 routes provides the same variety of challenge, from family rides to full-blown mountain adventures.

ISBN 0 948153-13-X **£7.50**

North Wales

PETE BURSNALL

A long awaited guide. 26 excellent and varied routes, circling some of North Wales' most beautiful lakes, criss-crossing wide stretches of forest, and reaching the highest points. Great attention has been paid to access, and both local authorities and land-owners have been exhaustively consulted.
Routes range from 10 to 60 km in length and cater for the family outing and the super-fit.

ISBN 0 948153-18-0 **£7.50**

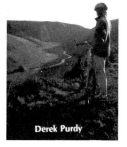

Northumberland

DEREK PURDY

32 well researched, totally legal routes throughout Northumberland, the best kept mountain biking secret in England. Bridleways, forest tracks, old drove-roads, ancient commercial routes, and neglected country roads.
Each route beautifully illustrated with black and white photos, two-colour maps, accompanied by technical terrain analysis and plotting plan, clearly written route descriptions including a little local history and colour.
There are routes for all abilities.

ISBN 0 948153-16-4 **£7.50**

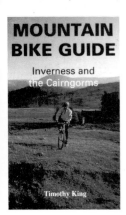

Inverness and the Cairngorms

TIMOTHY KING

21 routes characterised by the splendour of the scenery and by the variety of terrain.

Each has been thoroughly researched by the author who has consulted widely with local authorities, forestry groups and landowners.

Clear route maps and descriptions make for worry-free days, and each route is graded for length, amount of ascent, surface conditions and degree of remoteness.

Road and rail access for each route are detailed as are facilities at adjacent towns. Routes of 15km low level for family parties; and others of plus 50km over high ground for the fit.

ISBN 0-948153-35-0

£6.95

Wall Repairs

A NECKLACE OF SLINGS

DAVE GREGORY

Dave Gregory has been climbing for over forty years and writing stories for nearly as long. This collection of stories covers a broad spread over a wide canvas - rock climbing, the secret service, whimsy, ghosts, the perils and pleasures of skiing, Cairngorm white-out, Welsh vengeance. Which are fact and which are fiction. You will have to decide.

ISBN 0-948153-37-7   £15.00

ARKA TAGH

WILLIAM HOLGATE

This is the story of a determined but often troubled expedition into one of the last unexplored regions on earth. Isolated by the Taklamakan Desert to the north and the Tibetan wastes to the south, the region has remained largely ignored since the desperate forays of a handful of Victorian explorers. The book captures the tensions and dangers of the expedition's progress. *"It's probably the hardest area in the world to get to - Bill Tilman and I had hoped to get there but it is too far in"* - Eric Shipton.

ISBN 0-948153-33-4   £15.95

Over the Hills
& Far Away

Rob Collister

ROB COLLISTER

This collection of mountaineering essays ranges from the Welsh hills to the
Antarctic, and from the Alps to the Himalaya. Throughout it is imbued with the
spirit of self-sufficiency, adventure and good companionship. Conservation of
wild lands is also a constant theme.

ISBN 0-948153-40-7   £11.95.   Collector's Edition £16.00

*'In this collection of twenty-eight essays and three poems, written over a thirty year period, mountaineering
emerges not only as a lot of fun, but as something with moral content, and if that sounds heavy, rest
assured that Collister's writing is never heavy. All these essays are well crafted and well worth reading,
many are a joy to read, and the rest are good enough to anthologise'.*

Phil Bartlett - 'Climber'

May the fire be always lit

a biography of **JOCK NIMLIN**

ids thomson

I.D.S. THOMSON
Jock Nimlin was a legend among Glasgow's working-class climbers of the 1920s and 30s and a stalwart of the Harland & Wolff yard during the 1939-45 war. He went on to become the National Trust for Scotland's first field officer.
ISBN 0-948153-39-3   £11.95   Collector's Edition £16.00

This is an important book recording not just the considerable mountaineering achievements of a leading light in the Glasgow working class movement, but also, and perhaps most importantly, his innovatory lifestyle and attitudes. I cannot overstate the influence this philosophy had and still has on generations of Scottish climbers. Moreover much of this material has hitherto been inaccessible and Thomson has to be congratulated on his organisation of it into a very readable book.

Dave Brown 'Climber'.